NATIONS OF THE WORLD

FRANCE

Richard Ingham

Raintree

www.raintreepublishers.co.uk
Visit our website to find out more information about Raintree books.

To order:
☎ Phone 44 (0) 1865 888113
🗎 Send a fax to 44 (0) 1865 314091
💻 Visit the Raintree bookshop at www.raintreepublishers.co.uk to browse our catalogue and order online.

First published in Great Britain by Raintree, Halley Court, Jordan Hill, Oxford, OX2 8EJ, part of Harcourt Education Ltd.
Raintree is a registered trademark of Harcourt Education Ltd.

Produced for Raintree by the Brown Reference Group plc
Editor: Robert Anderson
Designer: Joan Curtis
Picture Researcher: Brenda Clynch
Editorial Assistant: Roland Ellis
Index: Kay Ollerenshaw

Raintree Publishers
Editors: Isabel Thomas and Kate Buckingham

Printed and bound in Singapore.

ISBN 1 844 21468 0
07 06 05 04 03
10 9 8 7 6 5 4 3 2 1

British Library cataloguing in publication data
Ingham, Richard
    France – (Nations of the world)
    1. Human geography – France – Juvenile literature
    2. France – Geography – Juvenile literature
    I. Title
    914.4

A full catalogue is available for this book from the British Library.

Acknowledgements
Front cover: Grape harvester carrying pail
Title page: A French market

The acknowledgements on page 128 form part of this copyright page.

Every effort has been made to contact copyright holders of any material reproduced in this book. Any omissions will be rectified in subsequent printings if notice is given to the publishers.

Contents

Foreword

Since ancient times, people have gathered together in communities where they could share and trade resources and strive to build a safe and happy environment. Gradually, as populations grew and societies became more complex, communities expanded to become nations – groups of people who felt sufficiently bound by a common heritage to work together for a shared future.

Land has usually played a important role in defining a nation. People have a natural affection for the landscape in which they grew up. They are proud of its natural beauties – the mountains, rivers and forests – and of the towns and cities that flourish there. People are proud, too, of their nation's history – the shared struggles and achievements that have shaped the way they live today.

Religion, culture, race and lifestyle, too, have sometimes played a role in fostering a nation's identity. Often, though, a nation includes people of different races, beliefs and customs. Many have come from distant countries, and some want to preserve their traditional lifestyles.

Nations have rarely been fixed, unchanging things, either territorially or racially. Throughout history, borders have altered, often under the pressure of war, and people have migrated across the globe in search of a new life or of new land or because they are fleeing from oppression or disaster. The world's nations are still changing today: some nations are breaking up and new nations are forming.

France is one of the world's oldest nations, with an independent history that dates back to the 5th century. Over the centuries, the French have developed a culture of remarkable richness and continuity. With the great revolution of 1789, France set out the programme of democratic ideals that still underpins many Western societies today. Nevertheless, France is not quite as uniform as it first appears. Historically, its regions have been home to minority cultures that challenged the supremacy of the capital, Paris. More recently, too, the life of its cities has been enriched by immigrants from Arab and African nations.

Introduction

France lies at the heart of western Europe. To the north are Belgium and Luxembourg; to the east, Germany and Switzerland; to the south-east, Italy and the independent **principality** of Monaco and to the south, the Mediterranean Sea, Spain and the tiny principality of Andorra, high up in the Pyrenees Mountains. The western boundary is the Atlantic Ocean, while to the north-west, a narrow arm of the Atlantic separates France from Britain. The British call this the English Channel. For the French, it is La Manche (The Sleeve).

France is a spacious country with a varied landscape and temperate climate. There are low-lying plains and lofty mountains, picturesque river valleys graced with fairytale palaces and lonely moorlands dotted with ancient standing stones. There are romantic old cities, busy ports and glamorous, sunny beach resorts.

France is also a very wealthy country. Its economy is fifth in the world league of richest countries in terms of **gross national product** (GNP). The standard of living – as measured by such factors as life expectancy, living space, quality of health care, diet and education – ranks sixth highest in the world.

Through its great size, economic and political weight and long history, France has helped shape the course of world events. The French Revolution of 1789, which overthrew the French **monarchy** and gave rise to a

Modern France has its roots in traditional country towns such as Bonnieux, Provence, dependent on surrounding crop land or pasture for its livelihood.

FACT FILE

● France covers some 551,204 sq km (212,820 sq miles), which makes it western Europe's biggest country by area. The UK is less than half the size of France.

● France forms a natural compartment of land on the map of Europe, bordered by mountains and sea. This fact helped its inhabitants become the first people in western Europe to form a **nation state**.

● France stands at a cultural crossroads of Europe – between the northern civilizations of the UK and Germany, on the one hand, and the Mediterranean cultures of Italy and Spain, on the other.

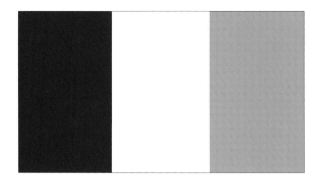

The French tricolore, France's national flag, was adopted during the early stages of the 1789 revolution when it was thought that France might retain its king and become a constitutional monarchy. White was the colour of the king, while red and blue were the colours of the French capital, Paris.

republic based on democratic ideals, stands as a key event in the making of the modern world. In addition, French culture has left its mark on every continent – in language, the arts, politics and science.

When we refer to France, we usually mean metropolitan France – the country that is part of continental Europe together with the Mediterranean island of Corsica. There are also extensive overseas territories that remain from France's colonial empire. These include the tropical islands of Guadeloupe and Martinique in the Caribbean Sea, French Guiana in South America and the island of Réunion in the Indian Ocean (see pages 30–1).

LANGUAGE AND PEOPLE

France is a republic. The head of state is President Jacques Chirac, a conservative who was first elected in 1995 and re-elected in 2002. The state flag is called the *tricolore*, or tricolour, because it has three vertical bands of blue, white and red. Until January 2002, the national currency was the French franc, written FF. The franc was then replaced by the **euro**, the currency of the European Union (EU).

The official language of France is French, which is spoken and

Before they were phased out in 2002, French franc notes depicted famous French people from history and the arts. The 20FF note, for example, showed the composer Claude Debussy, while the 50FF note had the 'Little Prince' and his creator, Antoine Saint Exupéry.

POPULATION DENSITY

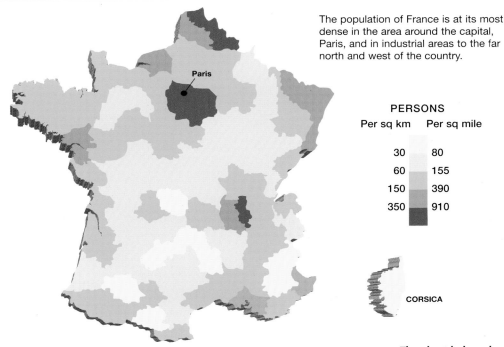

Paris

The population of France is at its most dense in the area around the capital, Paris, and in industrial areas to the far north and west of the country.

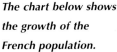

PERSONS

Per sq km	Per sq mile
30	80
60	155
150	390
350	910

CORSICA

taught everywhere. There are also significant minorities who speak the ancient languages of Breton, Basque (or Euskara), Occitan (or Provençal) and Corsu, the language of Corsica. Breton is spoken in the more remote corners of the region of Brittany on the western coast. Basque can be heard in the Pyrenees Mountains in the south-west. Occitan, or Provençal, is a language from the south, while Corsu is closely related to Italian and is spoken widely on Corsica.

French was originally the language of the area around Paris in the north, and emerged as standard French around the time of the **Renaissance** in the 16th century. There are many

The chart below shows the growth of the French population.

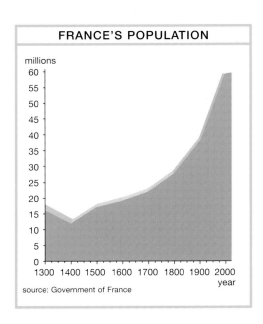

FRANCE'S POPULATION

millions

source: Government of France

year

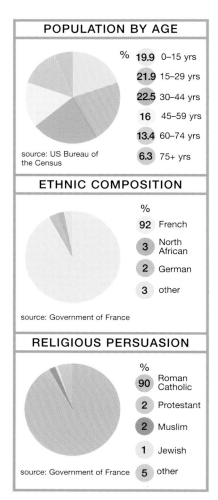

POPULATION BY AGE

%	
19.9	0–15 yrs
21.9	15–29 yrs
22.5	30–44 yrs
16	45–59 yrs
13.4	60–74 yrs
6.3	75+ yrs

source: US Bureau of the Census

ETHNIC COMPOSITION

%	
92	French
3	North African
2	German
3	other

source: Government of France

RELIGIOUS PERSUASION

%	
90	Roman Catholic
2	Protestant
2	Muslim
1	Jewish
5	other

source: Government of France

Above: *The French population is over-whelmingly white, with only tiny minorities of immigrant groups from former French colonies.*
Right: *The population was traditionally based in the countryside. This situation was reversed in the 20th century when farming declined.*

dialects, particularly in the border regions, where the French that people speak may be influenced by Flemish, German, Italian or Spanish. French is spoken not only by the citizens of France. People in neighbouring countries, such as Belgium and Switzerland, former colonies, such as Québec in Canada and Senegal in Africa, and overseas territories, such as Réunion, all speak French as their mother tongue. In all, there are about 90 million French speakers worldwide.

Population and religion

France has a population of about 60 million people. The population density is 111 people per square kilometre (286 people per square mile), which is less than half that of the UK or Germany but four times denser than that of the USA. The population is unevenly distributed and is concentrated in the north and south-east. Immigrants comprise about 7 per cent of the people and help compensate for an ageing population.

Nearly three-quarters of French citizens now live in towns and cities, compared with little more than half just after World War Two (1939–45). Despite big subsidies from the EU, agricultural incomes have declined, and over the past 30 years, millions of farmers have left the land. This has been a traumatic change for a country whose heart still lies in the countryside.

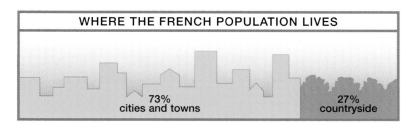

WHERE THE FRENCH POPULATION LIVES

73% cities and towns

27% countryside

France has no official religion. The French **state** and the Roman Catholic Church separated in 1905, and the influence of religion has declined in public and private life ever since. Religion cannot be taught in public schools, for example. Ninety per cent of French people are Roman Catholics, but the great majority of them do not go to church regularly.

The large community of Arab immigrants from North Africa has made Islam France's second-largest religion. Other major religions found in France are Judaism and Buddhism. At 600,000, the Jewish community – based largely in Paris – is the largest in Europe outside Russia. The Protestant and Orthodox Christian denominations are also represented.

Symbols and mottos

The symbol of the French Republic is **Marianne**. She is always shown as a woman wearing a Phrygian cap, which resembles a kind of long cap worn at the time of the French Revolution. As an emblem of the people, Marianne appears on French euro coins and postage stamps. Her face and figure are regularly updated and are now chosen by the public in an opinion poll. The faces of former film star Brigitte Bardot and actress Catherine Deneuve have both appeared as Marianne.

The motto of the French Republic, reputedly devised by American writer and inventor Benjamin Franklin, is '*Liberté, Égalité, Fraternité*' ('Freedom, Equality, Brotherhood'). This motto can be seen on public buildings and on French euro coins.

The national anthem

France's stirring national anthem, the 'Marseillaise', is a product of the French Revolution. It was composed in 1792 by Claude-Joseph Rouget de Lisle (1760–1837), and was named after troops from Marseille who first took up the tune. There are seven verses, but usually people perform only the first one, together with the chorus. Here is a translation of the first verse:

Forward, children of
the Fatherland.
The day of glory is near.
Tyranny stands before us.
The blood-stained banner
is raised.
The blood-stained banner
is raised.
Do you hear those ferocious
soldiers bellow in
our countryside?
They are coming to you
To cut the throat of your sons
and companions.
[CHORUS]
Citizens, take up arms!
Form your battalions!
Let us march forward, and may
a foul blood
Stain our fields!

Land and cities

'We [the French] have something of both the hot and cold regions ... so that in my opinion there is no other country so well situated as France.'

15th-century French historian Philippe de Commynes

The French sometimes describe their country as *l'Hexagone* (the Hexagon) because it is shaped like a six-sided polygon. With the exception of the north-eastern frontier, France is bordered by either towering mountains or oceans and seas, providing its people with excellent natural defences. The flat lands of Germany, Belgium and Luxembourg that share a border with France have always been vulnerable to attack, and France has been repeatedly invaded across this frontier.

Within these borders is an amazingly rich variety of landscapes. To the north are plains planted with wheat as well as forested tablelands, and in the south are the jagged peaks of the Pyrenees. In the far north-west is the rugged coast of Brittany, and in the south-east, the majestic Alps, with their dizzying peaks and icy blue lakes.

In between are the lush river valleys such as the Loire and the Rhône, with their slopes planted with hectares of vineyards, the sombre moors of inland Brittany and the desolate drifting dunes of Les Landes, the wooded pasture land and orchards of Normandy and the sun-baked hills of Provence. Even a single region in France can have an astonishing variety of landscapes. Provence, for example, has a rocky coastline bordering the deep blue Mediterranean Sea and a wild and hilly hinterland. Between the two lies a narrow strip of lush crop land where fruits, vegetables and flowers are grown.

A field of sunflowers grows in the crop lands of Provence, a region otherwise known for its beautiful coastline and rugged, herb-scented hills.

TERRAIN

The French landscape is made up of three major land forms: massifs, which are the remains of ancient mountains that have been worn down over millions of years, the rugged peaks and troughs of the younger mountain ranges found in the south and east and the plains of the west and north.

Mountains and massifs

In the far south of the country, forming the border with Spain, are the Pyrenees, a spectacular chain of mountains that extends more than 450 kilometres (280 miles) from the wind-buffeted Atlantic Ocean to the warm Mediterranean Sea.

In the south-east, separating France from Switzerland and Italy, are the French Alps, part of a great **cordillera** (system of mountain ranges) that extends across southern and central Europe. The French Alps are some of the most rugged mountains in the world and include Europe's tallest mountain, Mont Blanc (see page 26), which is 4807 metres (15,771 feet) high.

North of the Alps are the gentler Jura Mountains, a chain of limestone peaks that follows France's eastern border north of Lake Geneva. The mountains got their name from the Gaulish word *jor,* meaning 'forest'. Numerous forests of oak, beech and fir cover their lower slopes. Geologists named the Jurassic Period (208 to 144 million years ago) after the mountains because of the fossils found there dating from this time.

Geologically speaking, the Pyrenees, Alps and Jura are young mountains in comparison to France's ancient massifs. These were pushed up more than 225 million years ago by the crunching of the European landmass. The most impressive is the Massif Central, which lies in the middle of France and covers nearly one-sixth of the entire country. A distinctive part of the massif is the Puy region – a moon-like landscape of extinct volcano cones, craters and mineral springs. North of the Massif Central

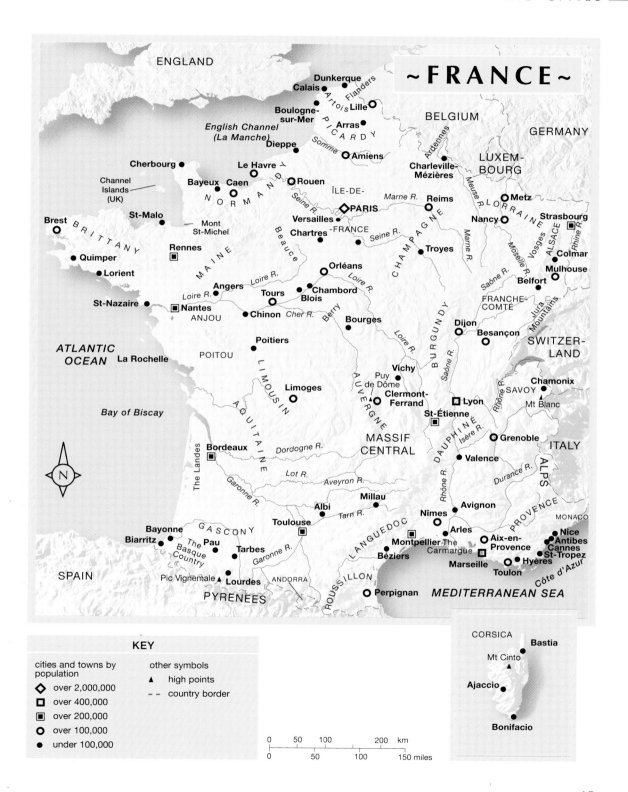

~FRANCE~

ENGLAND

Dunkerque
Calais
Boulogne-sur-Mer
Lille
Flanders
Artois
Arras
PICARDY
BELGIUM
GERMANY

English Channel
(La Manche)
Dieppe
Amiens
Somme
LUXEM-BOURG
Ardennes
Charleville-Mézières

Cherbourg
Le Havre
Rouen
ÎLE-DE-
Marne R.
Reims
Meuse R.
Metz
LORRAINE
Strasbourg

Channel Islands (UK)
Bayeux
Caen
N O R M A N D Y
Seine R.
PARIS
Versailles
-FRANCE-
Seine R.
Nancy
Moselle R.
Vosges
ALSACE
Colmar

Brest
B R I T T A N Y
St-Malo
Mont St-Michel
Beauce
Chartres
CHAMPAGNE
Troyes
Marne R.
Mulhouse
Saône R.
Belfort

Quimper
Rennes
M A I N E
Orléans
Loire R.
FRANCHE-COMTÉ
Jura Mountains

Lorient
Angers
Loire R.
Tours
Chambord
Blois
Loire R.
Dijon
Saône R.

St-Nazaire
Nantes
ANJOU
Chinon
Cher R.
Berry
Bourges
BURGUNDY
Besançon
SWITZER-LAND

ATLANTIC OCEAN
Poitiers
POITOU
Loire R.
Saône R.

La Rochelle
L I M O U S I N
Vichy
Puy de Dôme
AUVERGNE
Chamonix
SAVOY
Mt Blanc

Bay of Biscay
Limoges
Clermont-Ferrand
Rhône R.

A Q U I T A I N E
Lyon
St-Étienne
DAUPHINÉ
Grenoble
ITALY

Bordeaux
Dordogne R.
MASSIF CENTRAL
Isère R.
Valence
ALPS

The Landes
Lot R.
Aveyron R.
Durance R.

Garonne R.
Millau
Avignon
PROVENCE
MONACO

Albi
Tarn R.
Nîmes
Arles
Nice
Antibes

Bayonne
G A S C O N Y
Toulouse
Aix-en-Provence
Cannes

Biarritz
The Basque Country
Pau
Tarbes
Garonne R.
LANGUEDOC
Montpellier
Béziers
The Carmargue
Marseille
St-Tropez
Hyères
Toulon
Côte d'Azur

SPAIN
Pic Vignemale
Lourdes
PYRENEES
ANDORRA
ROUSSILLON
Perpignan
MEDITERRANEAN SEA

KEY

cities and towns by population

◇ over 2,000,000
□ over 400,000
▣ over 200,000
○ over 100,000
● under 100,000

other symbols

▲ high points
-- country border

0   50   100   200 km
0   50   100   150 miles

CORSICA
Bastia
Mt Cinto
Ajaccio
Bonifacio

is a low-lying area called the Paris Basin, whose flatness is interrupted only by isolated hills called *buttes*. The most famous *butte* is in Paris, the Butte de Montmartre, which is topped by the Sacré-Coeur **Basilica** (see page 43).

Other massifs include the Ardennes, a thickly wooded plain on the Belgian border, and the Vosges highlands, famous for their magnificent wild and rocky landscapes and pure mineral water.

Coastline and rivers

France is bound by four bodies of water: the North Sea, the Atlantic Ocean, the English Channel and the Mediterranean Sea. France's 3700 kilometres (2300 miles) of coastline are as varied as its interior landscape. On the northern coast along the Channel are spectacular chalky cliffs alternating with sandy beaches. Brittany, however, has a treacherous, rugged coastline where, over the centuries, many sailors have drowned. Further south, the Atlantic beaches are covered with fine sand, while those bordering the Mediterranean are pebbly.

There are four main rivers. The most important is the Rhine, of which 190 kilometres (118 miles) flow along France's border with Germany. The Rhine is a major transportation corridor. The Loire, at 1007 kilometres (626 miles), is France's longest river. It is very picturesque but is only partially navigable. The Rhône, which rises in Lake Geneva, Switzerland, flows 550 kilometres (342 miles) through France, where it is widely used by industry. The river joins with the Saône at the city of Lyon (see pages 46–7), where it is

The broad river Seine meanders across the great Paris Basin. The river is dotted with islands, such as the Île de la Cité in Paris and here at the town of Les Andelys, Normandy.

DEPARTMENTS AND REGIONS OF FRANCE

Metropolitan France is divided into 96 departments (*départements*). Most were formed at the time of the French Revolution and were often named after natural features such as rivers and mountains. The list below shows the number and name of each department, together with its capital. The numbers of the departments appear on all vehicle registration plates as well as in telephone codes.

The departments were grouped under 22 regions (*régions*) in 1972. As a part of the European Union (EU), France is also divided into eight EU regions.

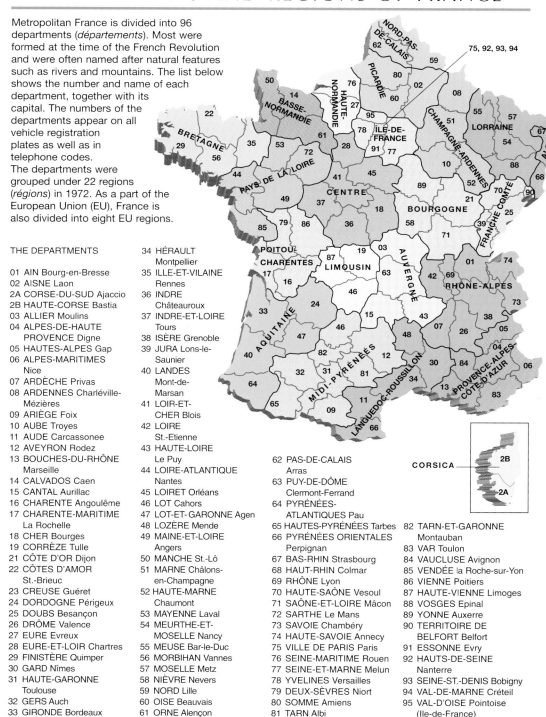

THE DEPARTMENTS

01 AIN Bourg-en-Bresse
02 AISNE Laon
2A CORSE-DU-SUD Ajaccio
2B HAUTE-CORSE Bastia
03 ALLIER Moulins
04 ALPES-DE-HAUTE PROVENCE Digne
05 HAUTES-ALPES Gap
06 ALPES-MARITIMES Nice
07 ARDÈCHE Privas
08 ARDENNES Charléville-Mézières
09 ARIÈGE Foix
10 AUBE Troyes
11 AUDE Carcassonee
12 AVEYRON Rodez
13 BOUCHES-DU-RHÔNE Marseille
14 CALVADOS Caen
15 CANTAL Aurillac
16 CHARENTE Angoulême
17 CHARENTE-MARITIME La Rochelle
18 CHER Bourges
19 CORRÈZE Tulle
21 CÔTE D'OR Dijon
22 CÔTES D'AMOR St.-Brieuc
23 CREUSE Guéret
24 DORDOGNE Périgeux
25 DOUBS Besançon
26 DRÔME Valence
27 EURE Evreux
28 EURE-ET-LOIR Chartres
29 FINISTÈRE Quimper
30 GARD Nîmes
31 HAUTE-GARONNE Toulouse
32 GERS Auch
33 GIRONDE Bordeaux

34 HÉRAULT Montpellier
35 ILLE-ET-VILAINE Rennes
36 INDRE Châteauroux
37 INDRE-ET-LOIRE Tours
38 ISÈRE Grenoble
39 JURA Lons-le-Saunier
40 LANDES Mont-de-Marsan
41 LOIR-ET-CHER Blois
42 LOIRE St.-Etienne
43 HAUTE-LOIRE Le Puy
44 LOIRE-ATLANTIQUE Nantes
45 LOIRET Orléans
46 LOT Cahors
47 LOT-ET-GARONNE Agen
48 LOZÈRE Mende
49 MAINE-ET-LOIRE Angers
50 MANCHE St.-Lô
51 MARNE Châlons-en-Champagne
52 HAUTE-MARNE Chaumont
53 MAYENNE Laval
54 MEURTHE-ET-MOSELLE Nancy
55 MEUSE Bar-le-Duc
56 MORBIHAN Vannes
57 MOSELLE Metz
58 NIÈVRE Nevers
59 NORD Lille
60 OISE Beauvais
61 ORNE Alençon

62 PAS-DE-CALAIS Arras
63 PUY-DE-DÔME Clermont-Ferrand
64 PYRÉNÉES-ATLANTIQUES Pau
65 HAUTES-PYRÉNÉES Tarbes
66 PYRÉNÉES ORIENTALES Perpignan
67 BAS-RHIN Strasbourg
68 HAUT-RHIN Colmar
69 RHÔNE Lyon
70 HAUTE-SAÔNE Vesoul
71 SAÔNE-ET-LOIRE Mâcon
72 SARTHE Le Mans
73 SAVOIE Chambéry
74 HAUTE-SAVOIE Annecy
75 VILLE DE PARIS Paris
76 SEINE-MARITIME Rouen
77 SEINE-ET-MARNE Melun
78 YVELINES Versailles
79 DEUX-SÈVRES Niort
80 SOMME Amiens
81 TARN Albi

82 TARN-ET-GARONNE Montauban
83 VAR Toulon
84 VAUCLUSE Avignon
85 VENDÉE la Roche-sur-Yon
86 VIENNE Poitiers
87 HAUTE-VIENNE Limoges
88 VOSGES Epinal
89 YONNE Auxerre
90 TERRITOIRE DE BELFORT Belfort
91 ESSONNE Evry
92 HAUTS-DE-SEINE Nanterre
93 SEINE-ST.-DENIS Bobigny
94 VAL-DE-MARNE Créteil
95 VAL-D'OISE Pointoise (Ile-de-France)

an important transport route to the Mediterranean Sea. Finally, there is the Seine, which is 774 kilometres (481 miles) long. It is a slow-moving river that flows through Paris before emptying into the English Channel at the busy port of Le Havre.

THE REGIONS OF FRANCE

For administrative purposes, France is divided into 96 *départements*. Each *département* is run by a *préfet*, who is appointed by the French president.

Each *département* is divided into a number of *arrondissements* (districts), which are further divided into numerous *cantons*.

The *cantons* are subdivided into *communes* (parishes), of which there are some 36,500 in France. The elected head of the *commune* is called the *maire* (mayor).

Historically, what is now called France was divided into a number of great regions or provinces (see page 52). These historical regions were often independent dukedoms (duchies), and their names are still used today to describe the broad cultural and geographic landscapes that make up this large, diverse country.

At the time of the French Revolution in the late 18th century, France was divided into administrative units called ***départements***, or departments. Today, there are 100 of these: 96 in metropolitan France (including the island of Corsica) and four overseas: Guadeloupe, Martinique, French Guiana and Réunion. In 1982, the departments were grouped under 22 *régions* (regions) and four *départements de outre mer* (overseas departments). These sometimes reflect the historical regions.

The north: Picardy, Artois and French Flanders

To the north of Paris is the windy plain that makes up the old provinces of Picardy, Artois and Flanders. The region is densely populated and heavily industrialized. The exploitation of the vast coal fields that run east to west through the region have created a bleak landscape of coal-mining waste and blast furnaces. The region also bore the brunt of the fighting during World War One (1914–18), when the battlefields around the Somme, Marne and Meuse rivers became a landscape of mud crisscrossed by trenches and barbed wire. Today, numerous cemeteries in the region commemorate the war dead.

Despite the damage inflicted by two world wars, the region has some lively and interesting cities and towns. Some, such as Arras, have vast marketplaces lined with tall Gothic buildings. Amiens has the largest medieval cathedral in France. The nave of the cathedral is 42 metres (138 feet) high and 145 metres (475 feet) long. Some say it is the most beautiful cathedral in France. Luckily, it survived the bombings in the two world wars that reduced the city to ruins. The coast is famous for its white cliffs and sand dunes. Two major ports, Boulogne and Calais, provide important ferry links with England. The undersea Channel Tunnel (see page 86) opened to passengers in 1994 and connects Calais to Folkestone in England.

Normandy and Brittany

These two regions on the western seaboard could not be more different. Normandy has two distinct zones. Upper Normandy, north of the Seine River, is primarily rich dairy land, while Lower Normandy, to the south

The Quiberon Peninsula on Brittany's southern coastline is buffeted by Atlantic storms. Its western, ocean-facing shore is so rugged and dangerous that it is called the Côte Sauvage (Wild Coast).

Mont Saint-Michel

Mont Saint-Michel is a granite rock that rises dramatically from the vast, glistening sand flats of Saint-Michel Bay on the border between Brittany and Normandy. Perched on top of the rock is the famous abbey of Saint-Michel.

At the beginning of the 8th century, the rock stood in the middle of a forest close to the coast. According to legend, a local bishop had a vision of the Archangel Michael commanding him to build a chapel on top of the rock. Shortly afterwards, the surrounding land fell into the sea, leaving the rocky mound stranded in a sandy bay.

In the 10th century, monks set up a monastery on the rock. When fortifications were added in 1256, workers had to haul huge blocks of granite over to the mound and drag them up a steep, winding track. Masons, sometimes working at dizzying heights, then set the blocks in place. During the Hundred Years' War (1337–1453), when the armies of the English King Henry V overran Normandy, Mont Saint-Michel alone was able to withstand the attack.

The abbey attracted many pilgrims, although reaching Mont Saint-Michel could be dangerous. Pilgrims could reach the rock only by walking over the treacherous shifting sands at low tide, and many people drowned. A causeway built in 1877 made crossing to the abbey safer and opened up the site to modern tourists.

and west of the Seine, tapers into a peninsula with a landscape of wooded hills and orchards. The green fields of western Normandy, arranged in a patchwork style known as *bocage*, are the home of France's most delicious butter and Camembert cheese. The capital of Normandy is Rouen, which has an old medieval centre.

Brittany, with its jagged coastline and lonely moorland interior, has a much wilder look. The region has always been set apart from the rest of France, both geographically and culturally. In the 6th century, a Celtic people related to those who settled in the UK came to the region, and until the 15th century, it was – at least in name – an independent dukedom. Even today, some Bretons fight hard to preserve their Celtic language (Breton) and traditions.

Life on the Breton peninsula is shaped by the sea. The economy has long been dependent on fishing. Today, though, tourism is equally important. The hot summers, particularly along Brittany's southern coast, make it a popular destination for French holidaymakers.

The Île-de-France

Île-de-France (Island of France) was the original 'France' before its kings gradually extended France to roughly its present-day size by the beginning of the 17th century. At the heart of the region is Paris, France's capital (see pages 36–45). Despite the growth of the capital's suburbs into the surrounding countryside, the region has many dense forests and agricultural lands as well as old and beautiful towns and cities.

In the south-east is the flat farmland of the Beauce. It is possible to see the spires of Chartres Cathedral (see pages 92 and 94–5) for kilometres across this plain.

Champagne, Alsace, Lorraine and Franche-Comté

To the north-east of the Paris Basin is the famous wine-growing region of Champagne. This is an area of gentle hills and winding rivers. Its northern border, where

Normandy's name comes from the Normans, a nickname for the Vikings, a Scandinavian people who conquered and settled the region in the 10th century.

Brittany's Celtic name was Armorica, which means 'land near the sea'.

The beautiful landscape of the Loire Valley, together with its temperate climate, made it popular with the French nobility, who built many beautiful and sumptuous country houses (châteaux) here. The most famous resident of the 16th-century château of Chenonceau (below) was Catherine de Medici, who lived here after the death of her husband, King Henry II, in 1559.

France meets Belgium, is covered by dense woodland, known as the Ardennes. The region's traditional capital is Reims, famous for its amazing network of champagne cellars, some of which run for 18 kilometres (11 miles).

The regions of Alsace and Lorraine lie on either side of the Vosges mountain range. Both are densely populated and heavily industrialized. Lorraine has rich deposits of coal and iron, while in Alsace, textile and chemical industries cluster along the Rhine.

Alsace and Lorraine were often sources of conflict between France and Germany. They became French in 1648, but the Germans took them back in 1871. They became part of France again only after World War One. Since 1919, they have remained French except for the German occupation during World War Two (1939–45). Although the people are proudly French, there is a strong German influence in the towns and villages, with their ornate, timbered houses, balconies, leaded windows and window boxes. The capital of Alsace is the large,

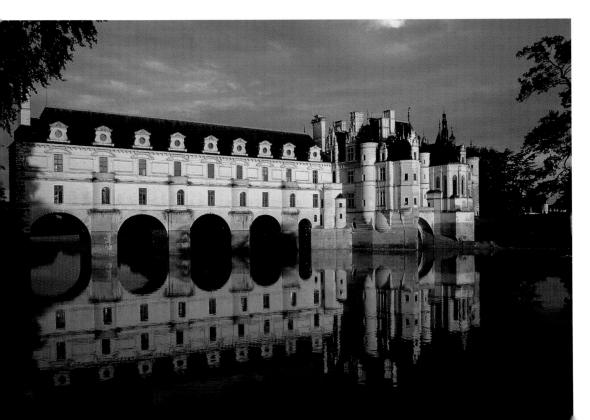

lively river port of Strasbourg. It is the only French city on the Rhine and it is the seat of the European Parliament and the Council of Europe.

To the south of Alsace and Lorraine lies the semi-mountainous agricultural region of Franche-Comté. It has many fast-flowing rivers and large lakes. The cream-coloured cows with reddish patches of this area produce the milk for the tasty and world-famous Gruyère cheese.

Maine, Anjou and Poitou

To the south-west of the broad Paris Basin, a series of low plains succeed one another along the Loire Valley. These provide the landscape for some of France's most famous and most visited regions. In the northern-most part, south of Lower Normandy, is the wooded region known as Maine, of which the capital, Le Mans, is renowned for its annual 24-hour motor race.

To the south-east is the agricultural region of Anjou. The lowland areas around the middle Loire Valley grow some of France's finest white wines. On the Loire's picturesque banks are many fine châteaux: some are grim fortresses; others are fairytale palaces (see box above).

To the south of Anjou is another flat agricultural region – Poitou. This, however, has a very different appearance. The house roofs feature bright, red tiles – unlike the grey slates of Anjou – goats graze in the fields

Châteaux of the Loire

Clustered along the fertile banks of the Loire River are some of France's most famous châteaux. During the Middle Ages, châteaux were fortified castles with a moat and drawbridge or were sometimes set high on a hill. A lord or knight lived in the castle and ruled over his domain – the surrounding territory granted to him by the king in return for military service.

From the 15th century, however, châteaux were more likely to be luxurious country houses than castles. The wealthy and leisured nobility who lived in them generally had more time for hunting and feasting.

Some of the châteaux of the Loire look like fairytale palaces. One of the largest and most famous, at Chambord, was the hunting 'lodge' of the French King Francis I. Built in the 16th century, it has huge round towers with conical tops, spectacular chimneys, coloured marble staircases and no less than 440 rooms.

and market gardens produce colourful fruit and vegetables, including the famous local green beans. The capital of Anjou is Angoulême. Poitou's capital is Poitiers.

The south-west: Aquitaine and the Landes

The old region of Aquitaine stretches from the Massif Central westwards to the Atlantic and south-west to the Pyrenees and the border with Spain. Its dramatic countryside is watered by a series of mighty and largely navigable rivers – the Dordogne, the Lot and the Garonne – which all flow into the Garonne Estuary.

The areas through which each river flows are very different. The Dordogne Valley is lush and fertile and home to some of France's best wines – collectively called Bordeaux after the city that stands at the mouth of the Garonne River. Some of the earliest signs of human habitation in Europe have been found around the Dordogne, notably the extraordinary cave paintings at Lascaux, dating back some 17,000 years (see page 50).

The river Lot is wilder. As the river twists and turns, it passes through deep gorges and beneath gloomy fortresses perched on rocky pinnacles.

Unlike the Lot and the Dordogne, the Garonne River flows down from the Pyrenees. It is a stately river, making great loops through a broad, fertile plain. Soft fruits, such as peaches and plums, grow here in abundance, and towards Bordeaux the river banks are home to what many people consider the greatest wines in France – white Sauternes and red Graves. On the river is the ancient city of Toulouse. French people call the city the *Ville Rose* (Pink City) because of the colour of the brick used in the local buildings.

To the south of Bordeaux, alongside the Atlantic, is a very different area. This is the Landes, a triangle of pale sand dunes and dark pine forests. Further south is the Pays Basque (Basque country), most of which lies across the border in Spain. The Basque people have a strong independent culture and speak a language unrelated to

The Basque people of France call their homeland Euskal-herri and their language Euskara.

While many Spanish Basques want an independent country, very few French Basques want to secede from (leave) France.

any other language spoken today. The area has a beautiful coastline of sandy coves and rocky headlands. The elegant resort of Biarritz attracts many visitors.

The wooded landscape of the Massif Central is studded with the pinnacles and cones of extinct volcanoes.

The Massif Central and the Auvergne

At the heart of France, west of the Rhône Valley, is a high, granite plateau called the Massif Central (see page 14). After the Alps and the Pyrenees, this is the third-highest part of France. The plateau has many deep craters and high rocky outcrops, a reminder that, millions of years ago, it was a volcanic area.

The heart of the region, called the Auvergne, is made up of pasture and woodland. The capital of the Auvergne, the industrial city of Clermont-Ferrand, has a 13th-century cathedral built of black lava rock. Over the city looms the dramatic Puy de Dôme, a 1464-metre (4803-foot) extinct volcano.

Burgundy and the Rhône Valley

Bridging the north and the south of France is the Rhône Valley, the heart of the great winemaking region of Burgundy. The vineyards on either bank of the Rhône produce some of France's most famous red and white wines, including Macon and Châteauneuf-du-Pape.

At the northern end of the valley lies Dijon, the historic capital of Burgundy. The city is famous for its numerous Gothic and **Renaissance** churches and also for its strong mustard. Further south is the bustling, industrial city of Lyon (see page 46), France's second-biggest urban area after Paris.

As the Rhône flows southwards, the countryside and its towns become more southern European in appearance. The valley is broader and there are many towns with ancient Roman ruins such as Vienne and Orange.

Mont Blanc: Europe's highest mountain

The summit of Europe's highest mountain, Mont Blanc – the name means 'white mountain' – lies just inside the French border with Italy. The mountain is 4807 m (15,771 ft) high and much of it is covered with the glaciers that give it its name. The first person to reach the summit was a doctor from the local town of Chamonix, who made his ascent in 1786.

Savoie and Dauphiné

These mountainous regions in the French Alps offer some of France's most spectacular scenery. There are snowy mountain peaks, dark forests, ice-blue lakes, dramatic waterfalls and roaring rivers. In winter, ski resorts such as Chamonix are popular tourist destinations.

The industrial city of Grenoble is surrounded by mountains. It is an important nuclear research centre. Just to the north-east of the city is the huge, circular 'Synchrotron' (particle accelerator).

Provence

In southern France, next to the Mediterranean Sea, is an oblong area of mostly hilly and mountainous land. Inland the rugged countryside is carpeted with wild flowers in spring. In the dry, hot summer months, the air is scented with wild thyme and buzzes with the song of the cicada.

The narrow strip of land between the dry hills and the bright blue sea, and in particular the stretch known as the Côte d'Azur (Blue Coast), has some of the most idyllic scenery in France. Its glamorous resorts such as Cannes (see page 105), Nice (see page 85) and Saint-Tropez have become the favourite haunts of writers, painters and film stars. They boast beautiful villas, elegant casinos and palm-fringed promenades.

By contrast, the large, modern port of Marseille (see page 47) has a lively mixture of French, Italian and North African cultures. Beyond Marseille, at the western end of Provence, is a triangle of salt marshes and lagoons called the Camargue (see page 28). At Provence's eastern edge is the tiny independent **principality** of Monaco.

One of the most famous sights in Provence is Mont Ste-Victoire. This 945-metre (3100-foot) high limestone mountain lies just east of the town of Aix-en-Provence. According to the light and time of day, it can appear blue, violet, pink or grey. French artist Paul Cézanne (1839–1906) painted and drew the mountain more than fifty times.

The Camargue

Between the two mouths of the Rhône River, next to the Mediterranean Sea, lies the Camargue, a flat, swampy area covering 787 sq km (304 sq miles). The Camargue is famous in France for its wild beauty and the variety of its wildlife. At the heart of the Camargue is a lagoon and nature reserve called the Étang de Vaccarès.

Much of the Camargue is made up of salt flats. During the winter, heavy rains flood the salt flats to a depth of 20–80 cm (8–32 in). In spring, the water levels fall and the swamps become covered with glasswort, a salt-loving plant that provides food for the many animals that graze there. In summer, the plains dry out and crack in the intense heat. The Camargue

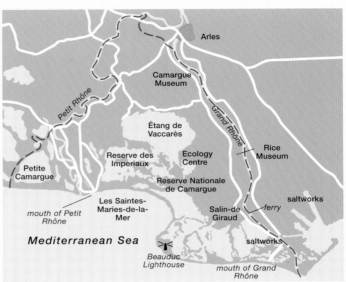

is the only place in France, and one of the few in the Mediterranean area, where the pink flamingo will nest. The Camargue's other famous residents include the small white Camargue horse (see photograph) – an animal that lives nowhere else in the wild – and the *biou*, a black bull.

Few people live in the Camargue. The principal settlement is the medieval fishing village of Les Saintes-Maries-de-la-Mer, which means 'Saint Marys of the Sea'. According to legend, Mary Magdalen and two other biblical women also named Mary, together with their servant, Sarah, landed here in the 1st century AD. Romanies (Gypsies) particularly honour Sarah, who was said to have had dark skin like their own.

Every year, Romanies from all over Europe gather in the village in honour of their patroness. On 25 May, they take statues of Sarah and two of the Marys from the church and carry them out to sea on a boat. There the Romanies call out 'Goodbye to the saints' before carrying the statues back to the church.

The island of Corsica

The wild, mountainous island of Corsica became part of France in 1769. It is the fourth-largest island in the Mediterranean Sea and lies 169 kilometres (105 miles) south of the French coast and only 90 kilometres (56 miles) west of Italy.

The Corsicans speak their own Romance (**Latin**-based) language, which is much closer to Italian than to French. They are fiercely proud of their culture and some of them resent French rule. A terrorist group frequently carries out bombings and kidnappings in an attempt to oust the French from the island.

North-western Corsica is mountainous. The highest peak, Mount Cinto, is 2710 metres (8890 feet) high. Towards the south-east, there are fertile plains. The island is covered with dense scrubland called *maquis*, where wild flowers and herbs grow. The scent of these can perfume the whole island and surrounding sea. The *maquis* gave its name to the courageous French Resistance fighters, the Maquis, of World War Two (1939–45) because the movement was very active in Corsica.

In central Corsica, away from the sea, are jagged peaks, deep granite gorges and picturesque hilltop villages and towns.

French emperor Napoleon was born in the city of Ajaccio on Corsica's west coast in 1769 – the same year that the French took over the island from the Italian state of Genoa.

French overseas territories and departments

During the 18th and 19th centuries, France developed a world empire with colonies in South-East Asia, Africa and South America. In the 20th century, the vast majority of these countries won their independence. A few have remained in French hands, usually as overseas territories or as overseas departments.

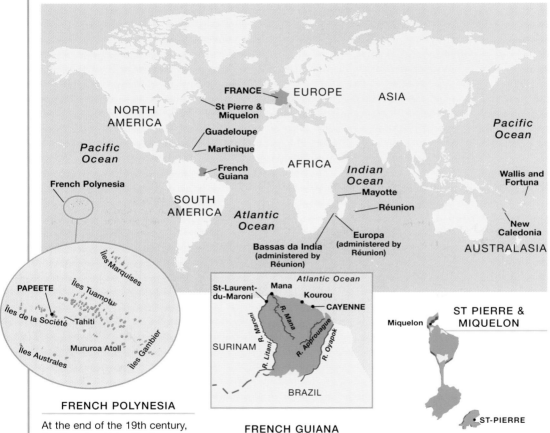

FRENCH POLYNESIA

At the end of the 19th century, the French painter Paul Gauguin painted Tahiti as an island paradise. Today, France uses this overseas territory largely for military purposes, notably nuclear testing on the Muroroa Atoll. The Polynesian majority is rarely consulted about what happens to the islands and today is demanding independence.

FRENCH GUIANA

The overseas department of French Guiana is the last remaining colony in South America. For a long time, France used the colony to imprison French convicts, most notoriously on Devil's Island. The majority of the colony's people are Creole (mixed French and African), but African and native peoples also live there.

ST PIERRE & MIQUELON

This barren archipelago (an area of water containing scattered islands) off the south coast of Newfoundland is all that is left of France's once extensive territory in North America. The French islanders traditionally survived by fishing, but today also rely on tourism. The capital, St-Pierre, is famous for its fine restaurants.

MARTINIQUE

Christopher Columbus called the mountainous, volcanic island of Martinique 'the most beautiful country in the world'. Today, it is an overseas department of France. The population is largely Creole or mixed and makes its living by agriculture or by tourism. There is tension between the majority and the descendants of the early French settlers (called Bekes), who account for 10 per cent of the population. Martinique is prone to natural disasters. In 1908, the Mount Pelée volcano erupted and completely destroyed the the port of St-Pierre.

RÉUNION

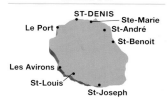

This island is one of France's overseas departments. It was originally uninhabited, so the French imported African slaves and, later, Indian labourers to work its sugar plantations. Today, there is tension between the poor black population and the richer French and Indian communities.

MAYOTTE

This densely populated island lies between Africa and Madagascar and is part of the fertile Comoros archipelago. The Arabs invaded Comoros in the 15th century and converted its inhabitants to Islam, which remains the island's main religion today. In 1975, Comoros, with the exception of Mayotte, became an independent country.

Today, the port of St-Pierre in the French overseas department of Martinique has been rebuilt and has become a popular tourist destination.

GUADELOUPE

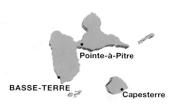

The tropical islands of Guadeloupe form another of France's overseas departments. The economy relies on the export of its banana crop and on tourism, but it also receives support from France and the EU. There is a strong independence movement among its mainly black and Creole population.

WALLIS AND FORTUNA

The people who live on these two tiny island groups are mainly Polynesian. Their traditional culture remains strong and the people grow just enough food to meet their own needs.

NEW CALEDONIA

The mainland – called Grande Terre (Big Land) – of New Caledonia (Nouvelle Calédonie) is a long, cigar-shaped island covered with mountains and surrounded by reefs. Grande Terre has rich mineral deposits and produces one-quarter of the world's nickel. There is a long history of violent tension between the poor and underemployed Melanesian native population (called the Kanaks) and the French community (called Caldoches).

THE CLIMATE

France's wide range of landscapes is mirrored by the diversity of its climate. Generally speaking, however, the climate is mild. More than half of the country has less than 80 days of frost annually, and most areas average 500 to 1250 mm (20 to 50 inches) of rain per year.

The west and north-west of the country are oceanic – that is, they have a temperate and humid climate that is shaped by the great cycles of weather that sweep in eastwards from the Atlantic. In coastal regions, such as Brittany, as much as 890 mm (35 inches) of rain can fall on 200 days of the year. The climate is ideal for cattle grazing, since it promotes the growth of grass.

Further inland, the rainfall is more modest. In the Paris Basin, the average yearly temperature is 12 °C (53 °F). Rainfall, at about 610 mm (24 inches) per year, is light. Large, treeless fields produce wheat and maize in abundance, as well as colza (a plant widely used as an oil in cooking) and sugar beet.

In the east of the country, a continental climate prevails – that is, the region has the same weather patterns as continental Europe, with icy but sunny winters and humid summers punctuated by rainstorms. Farming here is varied, although the weather is best suited for grain crops and white wine grapes grown on sunny, south-facing slopes in Alsace and Lorraine. Forestry, too, is an important industry (see page 82).

To the south, a Mediterranean climate prevails with hot, dry summers and warm, wet winters. Except for the Rhône Delta, the Mediterranean coastal belt is rocky and sandy and covered with scrub and cactus. It is not very fertile, although the clear

The weather of the French capital is influenced by both the Atlantic and continental climates. The sunny beach resorts of the Côte d'Azur, such as Nice and St-Tropez, enjoy a Mediterranean climate.

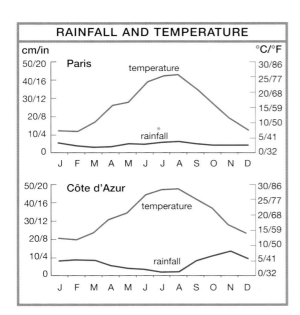

RAINFALL AND TEMPERATURE

skies and long, hot summers are good for growing tomatoes, peppers and other salad vegetables and for producing the grapes for strong red wines. Many Mediterranean farmers practise terracing – cutting into a hill-side to create flat areas for cultivation. This helps prevent the already poor soil from being eroded. Low rainfall and high temperatures from May to September in this area encourage the growth of wild herbs, such as thyme and rosemary, and olive and cork trees. Around Grasse, an area near the Italian border, farmers grow aromatic plants and flowers that are used in France's perfume industry (see page 90).

The other type of climate in France is particular to mountain areas. This type of climate has stark contrasts between winter and summer as well as higher precipitation (snow and rainfall). In the Pyrenees, the Alps and the highlands of the Jura near the Swiss border, frost and snow can last for several months in winter. In the western Pyrenees, one of France's wettest regions, rainfall can exceed 2030 mm (80 inches).

The mistral

The climate of southern France is usually excellent, but occasionally in winter and spring, a powerful chill wind blasts down the Rhône Valley towards the Mediterranean Sea. This wind is called the mistral, a name that comes from the Provençal word for 'master'. The mistral can sometimes reach speeds of more than 100 km/h (60 mph). This oppressive wind can linger for two or three days at a time and can make people feel upset and miserable.

WILDLIFE AND THE ENVIRONMENT

The French countryside and coastline are home to a rich variety of mammals, birds and reptiles. Wild boar and red and roe deer roam the forests, while in the eastern part of the country, there is a small number of wild cats.

In the mountains, there are two species of giant birds of prey, the French vulture and the royal eagle. Both are now rare. Each has a wing span of more than 2 metres (6½ feet). A pretty little deer called the chamois and the ibex, a large-horned relative of the goat, can sometimes be seen in the Alps.

France is home to 113 species of mammals, 363 species of birds, 30 varieties of amphibians, 36 kinds of reptiles and 72 kinds of fish, as well as 4200 species of plants and flowers.

33

Every spring, huge flocks of flamingos come to nest in the Camargue (see page 28). Some 14,000 pairs of flamingos spend the summer raising their offspring here before heading back to Africa.

The hot, dry summers of the south are an ideal environment for reptiles, such as lizards and tortoises. Huge flocks of pink flamingos live in the Camargue marshlands (see page 28) west of Marseille. The southern coast also harbours more exotic bird species such as the Egyptian vulture, the black-winged stilt and the bee-eater.

Environmental agencies work hard to ensure the survival of endangered species by reintroducing them to the wild. Their efforts often come into conflict with the interests of the tourism industry and with France's army of hunters. One particularly endangered animal is the Pyrenean brown bear, of which only about half a dozen are now left in the wild. Other endangered species are the lynx, the otter, the beaver and the white stork. The Atlantic salmon, threatened by overfishing, has been helped by the construction of special 'ladders' that enable spawning fish to swim upstream and breed.

The national and regional parks

France has six *parcs nationaux* (national parks), covering 0.7 per cent of the country's territory. Five of these are in mountainous regions. The Parc National des Pyrénées is popular with mountain climbers, while the Vanoise, Écrins and Mercantour national parks in the

Alps are important habitats for many species of wild animals and plants. The Parc National de Cévennes lies on the southern edge of the Massif Central. The Parc National de Port-Cros, an island off the Côte d'Azur, is famous for its rich marine life.

The national parks are administered directly by the national government and are carefully protected by the law. Dogs, vehicles and hunting are completely banned from them and tourism is very restricted.

In addition to the national parks, there are 33 *parcs naturels régionaux* (regional nature parks). These are locally managed and were established as a way of protecting natural habitats as well as boosting local tourism. There are important regional parks in Brittany, Corsica, Lorraine, Burgundy and the Camargue. All in all, more than 14,000 areas in France have been declared zones of **ecological** interest because of their rare and beautiful flora and fauna.

The French government first set up a ministry to oversee the environment in 1971. The ministry oversees the national parks, monitors pollution and works to protect the environment on a global scale.

The goat-like ibex is now a rare sight in the French Alps. Its close relative, the Pyrenean ibex, is also endangered. Other animals at risk of extinction in France include the Corsican deer, the brown bear, the river otter, Bonnelli's eagle and at least ten species of bats.

*Along the banks of
the river Seine in
Paris are tree-lined
cobbled embankments
called* quais. *On warm
summer days, people
come to stroll or to
sunbathe here. The*
quai *shown above is
on the Île St-Louis
and looks across to
its sister island, the
Île de la Cité, and the
spires and towers of
Nôtre Dame Cathedral.*

THE FRENCH CAPITAL: PARIS

For many people, the French capital, Paris, is simply the most romantic city in the world. Every year, tens of thousands of tourists visit the city. They may come to see and perhaps climb one of the world's most photographed landmarks, the Eiffel Tower, or to visit one of the city's many fine churches. They stroll along the cobbled embankments (*quais*) of the Seine, or take a trip down the river on a pleasure boat called a *bâteau mouche*.

Some tourists come to shop in the elegant boutiques of the world-famous Parisian fashion houses such as Chanel or Yves Saint Laurent, or to see the rich collections of art in Paris's many museums. Others may come for the delicious food and wine and the lively nightlife. People come to Paris for some or all of these things. One of the most enjoyable things to do in Paris, however, is to sit at one of its many pavement cafés and simply watch the world go by.

There is, however, another Paris. The capital and its sprawling suburbs are home to some 9 million people – nearly one-fifth of the French population. Only some

2 million, however, live in the Ville-de-Paris, the city of Paris proper. The majority live in the suburbs. Some suburbs are pleasant and prosperous, but others are grim and troubled by poverty, crime and racism.

Paris also has large immigrant communities – Arabs and Caribbeans from the former French colonies and Chinese. There is a long-standing Jewish community – the largest in western Europe – which has its heart in the historic quarter of the Marais. All these ethnic groups contribute to the life and culture of the city and some have given certain districts of the city a flavour of their own.

Last but not least, Paris is an important economic and industrial centre. The city hosts more international conventions than any other. Some 8000 foreign businesses have offices in the Paris region.

An overview of the city

The city of Paris is very compact – barely 10 kilometres (6 miles) at its widest – and is best explored on foot. For longer journeys, there is the *métro* (see page 42). This underground railway first opened in 1900 and today has fifteen lines running along some 198 kilometres (123 miles) of track.

The city is roughly oval in shape and is divided from east to west by the broad loops of the river Seine. To the north of the river is the Rive Droite (Right Bank) and to the south, the Rive Gauche (Left Bank). While each bank has its own special character, the two halves of the city are linked together by the many fine bridges over the river.

Paris is divided into twenty *arrondissements* (districts), which are known by their numbers. The first *arrondissement* is the area

Bridges old and new

The most famous bridge crossing the Seine is called the Pont Neuf (New Bridge), even though it is the oldest, dating from 1605. It crosses from the Left (southern) to the Right Bank, passing through the western tip of the Île de la Cité. The next bridge downstream is the romantic Pont des Arts (Bridge of the Arts). This 200-year-old iron footbridge crosses the river from the Louvre art gallery. Further downstream are other bridges, such as the grandiose Pont Alexandre III, built in 1900. It is festooned with gilded statues and lamps.

around the Louvre and Les Halles. From there, the *arrondissements* spiral out to reach the 20th district on the eastern side of the city. Paris is criss-crossed by many broad, straight roads known as boulevards. These were built in the second half of the 19th century, when much of the older Paris was demolished to make way for them.

From Nôtre Dame to the Eiffel Tower

The heart of the city – and the place where the city was founded – is two small islands on the Seine – the Île de la Cité (City Island) and the smaller Île St-Louis. On the Île de la Cité is one of the capital's most famous buildings – the cathedral of Nôtre-Dame. This cathedral, with its soaring towers and flying buttresses, was begun in 1163 and completed in 1345. It has many fine architectural features, such as three stained-glass rose (circular) windows.

Looking out from the roofs of Nôtre Dame Cathedral in Paris are grimacing gargoyles. These statues of ferocious-looking humans or animals are drains that carry away rainwater from the roofs of Gothic buildings.

The cathedral is also famous as the setting for the novel *Nôtre Dame de Paris* (*The Hunchback of Nôtre-Dame*) by French writer Victor Hugo (see pages 102–3). In this novel, the cathedral's roofs and towers are home to the kindly hunchback Quasimodo. Today, it is still possible to climb to the roof, which is decorated with monstrous heads called gargoyles. This position offers one of the finest views over Paris.

The intellectual and administrative districts of the city are on the Rive Gauche (Left Bank). The Latin Quarter is home to the city's oldest university, the Sorbonne (see page 112). The district got its name because, until the French Revolution, the students spoke Latin as their everyday language. The area is overlooked by the Panthéon – a

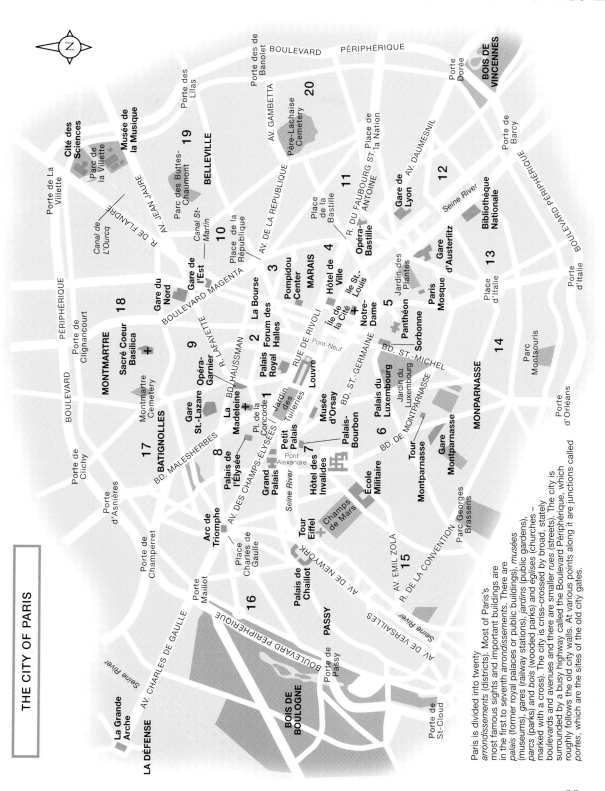

THE CITY OF PARIS

BOIS DE BOULOGNE

LA DÉFENSE

La Grande Arche

Seine River

AV. CHARLES DE GAULLE

Porte de Champerret

Porte Maillot

Porte d'Asnières

Porte de Clichy

Porte d'Auteuil

Porte de Passy

PASSY

Palais de Chaillot

AV. DE NEW YORK

Tour Eiffel

Champs de Mars

AV. DE VERSAILLES

Seine River

Porte de St-Cloud

BOULEVARD PÉRIPHÉRIQUE

Place Charles de Gaulle

Arc de Triomphe

AV. DES CHAMPS-ÉLYSÉES

16

Palais de l'Élysée

8

Grand Palais

Petit Palais

Pont Alexandre

Pl. de la Concorde

Jardin des Tuileries

Palais-Bourbon

Hôtel des Invalides

7

École Militaire

AV. EMIL ZOLA

R. DE LA CONVENTION

15

Parc Georges Brassens

Porte d'Orléans

BOULEVARD

Porte de Clignancourt

MONTMARTRE

Sacré Coeur Basilica

18

Montmartre Cemetery

17

BATIGNOLLES

BD. MALESHERBES

Gare St.-Lazare

9

Opéra-Garnier

La Madeleine

BD. HAUSSMAN

R. LAFAYETTE

1

Musée d'Orsay

Louvre

RUE DE RIVOLI

Forum des Halles

2

Palais Royal

La Bourse

PÉRIPHÉRIQUE

Porte de La Villette

Cité des Sciences

Parc de la Villette

Musée de la Musique

AV. JEAN JAURÈS

R. DE FLANDRE

Canal de L'Ourcq

Porte de Pantin

Gare du Nord

BOULEVARD MAGENTA

Gare de l'Est

Canal St-Martin

10

Parc des Buttes-Chaumont

19

Porte des Lilas

BELLEVILLE

Place de la République

AV. DE LA RÉPUBLIQUE

3

Pompidou Center

MARAIS

Hôtel de Ville

4

Île de la Cité

Pont-Neuf

Notre-Dame

Île St-Louis

BD. ST-GERMAINE

BD. ST-MICHEL

5

Panthéon

Sorbonne

Paris Mosque

Jardin des Plantes

Porte des Banolet

BOULEVARD

Porte de Banolet

AV. GAMBETTA

Père-Lachaise Cemetery

20

PÉRIPHÉRIQUE

Porte Dorée

BOIS DE VINCENNES

Porte de Barcy

AV. DAUMESNIL

Gare de Lyon

R. DU FAUBOURG ST. ANTOINE

Place de la Nation

Place de la Bastille

11

Opéra-Bastille

Seine River

Gare d'Austerlitz

12

Bibliothèque Nationale

13

BOULEVARD PÉRIPHÉRIQUE

Porte d'Italie

Place d'Italie

14

Parc Montsouris

MONPARNASSE

BD. DE MONTPARNASSE

Palais du Luxembourg

6

Jardin du Luxembourg

Tour Montparnasse

Montparnasse

Gare Montparnasse

Jardin des Plantes

Paris is divided into twenty *arrondissements* (districts). Most of Paris's most famous sights and important buildings are in the first to seventh *arrondissements*. There are *palais* (former royal palaces or public buildings), *musées* (museums), *gares* (railway stations), *jardins* (public gardens), *parcs* (parks) and *bois* (wooded parks) and *églises* (churches – marked with a cross). The city is criss-crossed by broad, stately boulevards and avenues and there are smaller *rues* (streets). The city is surrounded by a busy highway called the Boulevard Périphérique, which roughly follows the old city walls. At various points along it are junctions called *portes*, which are the sites of the old city gates.

39

The great avenue called the Champs-Elysées passes through some of Paris's most luxurious districts. Near it are some of the city's most important buildings, including the official residence of the French president and the Arc de Triomphe. At Christmas and New Year, the avenue is decorated with thousands of lights.

huge, church-like building that is the burial place of some of France's most distinguished citizens, including Victor Hugo and scientists Pierre and Marie Curie. Nearby is the Musée Nationale du Moyen-Âge (National Museum of the Middle Ages), which has displays of medieval sculptures and tapestries. The district also has one of the city's most elegant parks, the Jardin du Luxembourg (Luxembourg Gardens). On Sunday afternoons, people come to stroll along its formal pathways.

Further west along the river is the Musée d'Orsay. Until the 1980s, this grand, elaborate building was a railway station. Today, it holds one of the best collections of Impressionist art (see page 98) in the world.

Next along the river are the government buildings, including the Assemblé Nationale (National Assembly, see pages 71–3) and many government ministries. From here it is a short walk to the famous Tour Eiffel (Eiffel Tower), a tall, tapering construction of latticed ironwork. The view from the top on a sunny day or at night is worth the long trip up (see box opposite).

The Right Bank

On the Right Bank are the city's commercial and shopping districts. The Champs-Elysées is one of the most famous streets in the world. This ten-lane avenue is lined with expensive shops, car showrooms and restaurants. On Bastille Day (14 July), there is a military parade along the avenue to commemorate the 1789 revolution, and on New Year's Eve, there is always a huge street party.

The Champs-Elysées is more interesting, however, for the monuments that lie at either end of the avenue. At the northwestern end is the Arc de Triomphe. This majestic arch was originally designed to celebrate the military achievements of the French emperor Napoleon (1769–1821). After his final defeat in 1815, the triumphal arch was left incomplete and was later redesigned to honour those who fought in the 1789 revolution.

At the other end of the Champs-Elysées is another reminder of the revolution – the huge Place de la Concorde. During the **Terror** (see page 58) that followed the revolution, this was the site of the guillotine that took the lives of numerous victims, including those of King Louis XVI and his queen, Marie-Antoinette.

After the Terror ended, the square was given the name 'Concorde' ('harmony') in a spirit of national reconciliation. In the middle of the Place de la Concorde stands an ancient Egyptian monument today known as the Obelisk of Luxor. Like Cleopatra's Needle in London, this inscribed stone pinnacle was a gift from the viceroy of Egypt in the 1830s.

The Eiffel Tower

Until New York's skyscrapers were built in the 1930s, the Eiffel Tower was the tallest structure in the world. The tower is 300 m (984 ft) high and gets its name from Gustave Eiffel (1832–1923). He was the daring engineer who designed the tower for the 1889 World Fair. Three hundred workmen had to perform acrobatic feats to rivet its 12,000 iron struts together. At the time, many people thought the tower was an eyesore. Others welcomed it as a sign of things to come. It delighted the French poet Guillaume Apollinaire, who imagined the tower as a shepherd leading Paris into the 20th century.

The second level
Visitors to the second level have to climb another 700 steps or take another lift. This level has a restaurant named after the famous science-fiction writer Jules Verne.

The first level
The first platform is 57 m (187 ft) above the ground and is reached by a lift or 360 steps. A small cinema tells the history of the Eiffel Tower, including footage of some of the famous people, such as Charlie Chaplin and Adolf Hitler, who have visited the tower.

The third level
In the busy summer months, there is a long queue for the double-decker lifts that take visitors to the third and highest level. If it is a fine day, the views make the trouble worthwhile. The viewing platform is 271 m (899 ft) above the ground and can hold as many as 800 people at a time. On a clear day, it is possible to see for 72 km (45 miles).

Anywhere you go in Paris, there is always a métro (underground) station within five minutes' walk. The RER lines are fast rail lines that take commuters – and tourists – to and from the centre of Paris.

To the east of the obelisk is the Tuileries, another of Paris's graceful formal gardens. It was designed by 17th-century landscape designer André Le Nôtre, who also laid out the grounds of the king's luxurious palace at Versailles. Today, visitors to the gardens may find pony rides, *boules* players (see page 115) and, in summer, a big fair.

On the other side of the Tuileries is the huge former royal palace of the Louvre. Since the French Revolution, the palace has housed some of France's richest national art collections. There are ancient Greek and Roman antiquities, such as the beautiful winged statue of Nike of Samothrace, and a wealth of Chinese and Islamic art objects. Masterpieces of Renaissance art such as Leonardo da Vinci's *Mona Lisa* can also be seen here. Above all, there is the national collection of French art, ranging from exquisite still lifes by Jean-Baptiste

KEY	
▬▬	*métro* line and station
①	*métro* terminal and line number
○	interchange
▬▪▬	RER line and station

THE PARIS *MÉTRO*

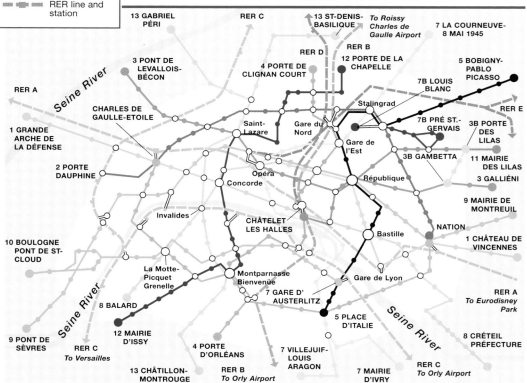

Chardin to epic master-pieces, such as Théodore Géricault's epic *Raft of the Medusa*. In 1992, the Louvre was remodelled and extended. Now there is almost enough room to display all the museum's rich treasures.

Further to the west, beyond the shopping mall of Les Halles – a former wholesale food market – is a high-tech, glass-fronted building called the Pompidou Centre. It is built on the site of the medieval Beaubourg – a name still applied to the surrounding area today. The Pompidou Centre houses the National Museum of Modern Art.

A little further east is a beautiful neighbourhood of narrow streets and old townhouses (*hôtels*) called the Marais. The area was once marshland (the French word *marais* means 'marsh'), but in the 16th and 17th centuries, it was drained and became a fashionable place for the aristocracy to live. Today, there are lots of smart shops, excellent museums – such as that devoted to the painter Pablo Picasso – a beautiful square called the Place des Vosges and the traditional Jewish quarter.

At the south-eastern corner of the Marais is the Bastille. The royal fortress stormed by the Paris mob in the French Revolution once stood on this site.

Away from the river, to the north and high up on a *butte*, is a busy area known as Montmartre, which was once popular with artists. On top of the hill, with a commanding view of Paris, is the white-domed Sacré Coeur (Sacred Heart) Basilica. At night, young people gather on the steps outside the church to chat, sing and play the guitar.

On the facade of the Pompidou Centre are glass-fronted escalators and viewing platforms and massive, colourful pipes. There are panoramic views over the rooftops of Paris, up to the Butte de Montmartre and the glistening white Sacré Coeur Basilica.

Right: Paris is a striking mix of the new and old. Here the 21-metre-high (69-foot) glass Louvre pyramid contrasts with the palace itself.

Below: The Grande Arche dominates La Défense, a district of skyscrapers and high-rise apartment blocks just west of Paris. The Grande Arche stands at one end of the 8-kilometre (5-mile) Grand Axe (Great Axis) – a row of monumental buildings and avenues that begins with the Louvre and includes the Concorde obelisk, the Champs-Elysées and the Arc de Triomphe.

The new Paris

French leaders – whether kings or presidents – have always liked to leave their mark on the Paris skyline. The most recent and enthusiastic builder was President François Mitterrand (1916–96). Among his projects were a huge glass pyramid built in front of the Louvre, a soaring new opera house at the Bastille, the monumental Grande Arche (Great Arch), which echoes the Arc de Triomphe, and a National Library, dominated by tall twin

towers. Many people have criticized these daring new additions to the beautiful Paris cityscape. Others praise them, arguing that a city cannot live only in the past.

The Paris region

There are many places within easy reach of Paris that are well worth a day's visit. There is a suburban rapid transit network called the RER (*Réseau Express Régional* – Express Regional Network) that makes getting to and from central Paris quick and easy.

The most famous sights are the royal palaces, including the extravagant 17th-century château of Versailles built for Louis XIV (see page 95) and the Renaissance château at Fontainebleau, where the French kings liked to hunt in the surrounding forest. Fontainebleau Forest is one of the most beautiful wooded areas in France. In the mid-19th century, painters such as Jean-Baptiste-Camille Corot and Jean-François Millet

PARIS REGION

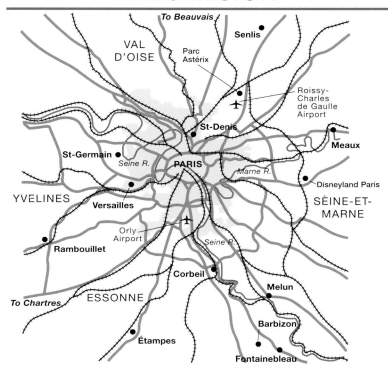

VAL D'OISE

To Beauvais

Senlis

Parc Astérix

Roissy-Charles de Gaulle Airport

St-Denis

Meaux

St-Germain

Seine R.

PARIS

Marne R.

Disneyland Paris

YVELINES

Versailles

SEINE-ET-MARNE

Orly Airport

Rambouillet

Seine R.

Corbeil

Melun

To Chartres

ESSONNE

Barbizon

Étampes

Fontainebleau

Left: *The rail network surrounding Paris brings many famous buildings and beautiful areas of countryside within easy reach.*

settled in the village of Barbizon in the forest. Their paintings show its landscapes of oak, beech and birch, its ponds and gorges and skies full of weather. Today, some of the artists' studios are open to the public.

The towns of Chartres and Beauvais have two of the most famous cathedrals of France (see pages 94–5). Closer to Paris is the St-Denis Basilica, the first Gothic building in France. Saint Denis was the first bishop of Paris, who lived in the 3rd century AD. According to legend, he was beheaded for his faith on the hill of Montmartre (Mount of the Martyr), but miraculously managed to stumble a few kilometres northwards to the spot where a church was later raised in his honour. In the basilica are the tombs of almost all the French kings.

Near Paris are two amusement parks: Euro-Disneyland and the Parc Astérix, devoted to the Gaulish hero of the French cartoon strip (see page 104).

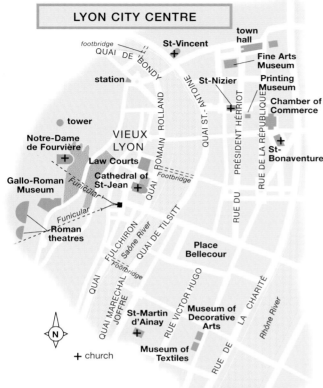

LYON CITY CENTRE

town hall

footbridge

QUAI DE BONDY

St-Vincent

station

St-Nizier

Fine Arts Museum

Printing Museum

Chamber of Commerce

tower

VIEUX LYON

QUAI ST.-ANTOINE

QUAI ROMAIN ROLLAND

RUE DU PRÉSIDENT HÉRRIOT

RUE DE LA RÉPUBLIQUE

Notre-Dame de Fourvière

Law Courts

St-Bonaventure

Gallo-Roman Museum

Funicular

Cathedral of St-Jean

Footbridge

QUAI FULCHIRON

Saône River

QUAI DE TILSITT

RUE DU

Funicular

Roman theatres

Place Bellecour

QUAI MARÉCHAL JOFFRE

Footbridge

St-Martin d'Ainay

Museum of Decorative Arts

RUE VICTOR HUGO

RUE DE LA CHARITÉ

Rhône River

N

Museum of Textiles

+ church

Lyon, like Paris, is divided into *arrondissements* (districts). Lyon has nine such *arrondissements*.

Lyon was the birthplace of the Lumière brothers, who pioneered cinema, and of the physicist André-Marie Ampère, after whom the unit of electricity is named – the amp.

BEYOND PARIS

In recent centuries, Paris has dominated the culture, politics and economy of France. However, regional capitals such as Lyon and Marseille are increasingly making their mark on both the national and international stage. In fact, these cities are reclaiming the larger historical role they enjoyed in the past.

Lyon

In terms of area, Lyon is the second-largest city in France. Its ancient centre lies between the Rhône and Saône rivers. From here, the city and its suburbs have sprawled far across the broad Rhône Valley.

The city was originally founded by Greeks in 54 BC and became the Roman colony of Lugdunum under Lucius Munatius Plancus in 43 BC. In the Middle Ages, it grew prosperous by manufacturing silks and other textiles and by holding trade fairs attended by bankers and merchants from all over Europe.

Today, the city remains a busy and business-oriented place. The centre of the city stands on a tongue of land between the Rhône and Saône rivers called the Presqu'ile (Peninsula). This district is dominated by the vast, gravel-covered Place Bellecour, which has a statue of Louis XIV on horseback at its centre.

Westwards, across the Saône, is the oldest and most picturesque part of Lyon – Vieux Lyon (Old Lyon). This is a district of rambling streets, narrow arched passages called *traboules* and quaint courtyards. Overlooking Vieux Lyon is the hill of Fourvière, on which there are two ancient Roman theatres. The largest was built by the Roman Emperor Augustus (63 BC–AD 14) and could hold 10,000 spectators.

Today, Lyon is most famous for its food. It is said that there are more restaurants here per square metre than anywhere else in the world.

Marseille

The ancient, bustling port of Marseille is, after Paris, the second most populated city of France. Its crowded streets are home to people from all over the Mediterranean: French, Italians and North Africans. The city is also one of the poorest in France and this poverty has sometimes led to racial tension.

The city is even older than Lyon. In ancient times the Greeks called it Massalia. Later the city became a powerful ally of Rome. During the Middle Ages, the city grew rich on the goods that passed in and out of its large harbour.

Marseille is not a beautiful city and there are few tourist sights. What attracts people to the city is its electric atmosphere. In the Vieux Port (Old Port), there are seafood restaurants selling the local fish stew called *bouillabaisse*.

To the north is the vibrant Arab district of Belsunce. In its streets people set up market stalls on cardboard boxes, selling everything from fragrant spices to the latest hi-fi equipment.

Marseille grew up around its port (the Vieux Port), which was protected by two massive forts.

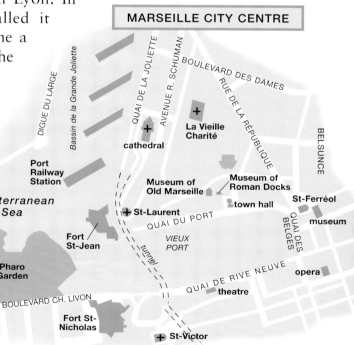

MARSEILLE CITY CENTRE

+ church

47

Past and present

'France is not France unless it has grandeur.'

20th-century French president Charles de Gaulle

France is home to the descendants of many different peoples. Paintings on the walls of a cave at Lascaux, near the Dordogne River in south-west France, give a glimpse of what life was like for the country's earliest-known inhabitants. These vivid paintings were made about 17,000 years ago. They tell us of a community of people who lived in caves and hunted wild animals. We also know that they gathered berries and fruit for food and used flints and other stone tools. Another remnant of **prehistory** are the standing stones and dolmens (stone tombs) of Brittany, the first of which were built about 6000 years ago. These monuments were erected by an ancient people who worshipped the sky and the land.

Later archaeological evidence tells of a succession of settlers and invaders who established themselves in France. The first written documentation that we have comes from the ancient Romans. They called the country we know as France, Gallia (Gaul), meaning the 'land inhabited by the Gauls'. The Gauls were a Celtic people who left their homelands in what is now Germany in about 1500 BC and migrated southwards and westwards. In 390 BC, the Gauls ransacked the great city of Rome.

In 121 BC, Rome went on the offensive against the troublesome Gallic tribes. The Romans crossed the Alps and set up a Roman province on France's Mediterranean coast – the present-day Provence. In 52 BC, the

A 14th-century manuscript shows the army of Frankish king Charlemagne (742–814) riding into battle against the Muslim rulers of Spain.

FACT FILE

- The name 'France' derives from the Franks – a powerful Germanic tribe that lived in the country from around the 3rd century AD.

- We sometimes use the word 'Gallic' to mean something typically French. 'Gallic' refers to the ancient land and people of Gaul, which covered roughly the area of modern France.

- The French sometimes date the foundation of their country from AD 486, when the Frankish leader Clovis defeated the Roman governor of France, Syagrius. In AD 508, Clovis made Paris the capital of the new kingdom of France.

A discovery at Lascaux

In 1940, four teenagers out on a walk discovered the Lascaux cave paintings when their dog fell down a hole. The hole was the entrance to caves, the walls of which were covered with painted and engraved images of animals. The paintings were in simple, bright colours – red, yellow and brown – as well as black. There were red deer, oxen and horses, as well as three magnificent aurochs, an extinct wild ox.

After the caves were discovered, they were opened to the public, but breath and body heat from the visitors caused the paintings to deteriorate. In 1963, the authorities ordered the caves to be closed to preserve the paintings. A replica cave was built close by so that visitors could see copies of the magnificent paintings.

Roman emperor Julius Caesar decisively defeated the Gallic army of Vercingetorix, and the whole of Gaul became part of the Roman empire.

Roman rule had a deep and lasting impact on Gallic culture. The language spoken in France today, for example, is a Romance language – that is, it developed from the **Latin** spoken by the Romans. It was during Roman times, too, that the people of Gaul first converted to Christianity.

From the 3rd century AD, Gaul came under attack from Germanic peoples from the north-east. At first, the Romans managed to tame the invaders and even used them as soldiers to defend the empire's frontiers. In the 5th century, however, the Roman empire collapsed, and Germanic tribes were left in control of much of the empire's western territories, including Gaul. The most powerful of these tribes were the Franks – who gave their name to France – and the Burgundians, who settled in the eastern areas of the country.

FRANCE IN THE MIDDLE AGES

The Frankish kingdom was at its height in the 9th century when Charlemagne (Charles the Great) extended Frankish rule over most of continental Europe. In Rome, on Christmas Day 800, the pope crowned Charlemagne emperor of the Holy Roman empire. Under Charlemagne's patronage, the monasteries led a revival of learning and art in France.

After Charlemagne's death, the Frankish empire broke up, and France became little more than a collection of small independent states. Vikings from Scandinavia seized the city of Rouen on the river Seine and set up a dukedom. The invaders were nicknamed Normans, or Northmen, and their dukedom was called Normandy. The most famous Duke of Normandy was William the Conqueror, who in 1066 invaded England, defeated its king, Harold, and seized the English throne.

By the time of the Frankish king Charlemagne's death in 814, his empire stretched over most of western Europe. Charlemagne's capital was not at Paris but at Aix-la-Chapelle, now Aachen, in Belgium.

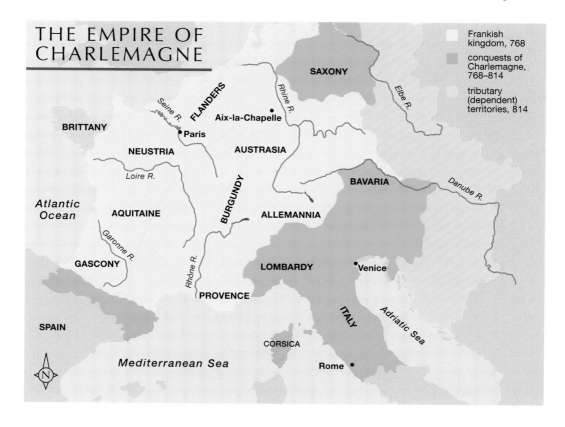

THE EMPIRE OF CHARLEMAGNE

Frankish kingdom, 768

conquests of Charlemagne, 768–814

tributary (dependent) territories, 814

SAXONY

Seine R.
FLANDERS
Rhine R.
Elbe R.
Aix-la-Chapelle
BRITTANY
Paris
NEUSTRIA
AUSTRASIA
Loire R.
BAVARIA
Danube R.
Atlantic Ocean
AQUITAINE
BURGUNDY
ALLEMANNIA
Garonne R.
Rhône R.
GASCONY
LOMBARDY
Venice
PROVENCE
SPAIN
ITALY
Adriatic Sea
CORSICA
Mediterranean Sea
Rome

N

THE GROWTH OF THE KINGDOM OF FRANCE

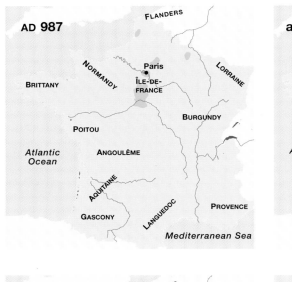

In the 10th century, France was little more than an 'island' of territory around Paris. Some 600 years passed before something like the country we call France was formed.

At the end of the 10th century, Hugh Capet founded a new dynasty of kings – the Capetians. At this time, much of the area that later became France was made up of a number of semi-independent provinces, such as Brittany and Provence. The provinces were ruled by powerful dukes who disliked interference from the king in Paris. Under the Capetians, French cities flourished and many beautiful Gothic cathedrals were built.

The last Capetian king died in 1328. His male child lasted only five days longer, and the French throne passed to the kings of the Valois dynasty. Their right to the throne was disputed by the English kings, who already ruled large areas of France, including Normandy and the rich south-western territory of Aquitaine. France was lucky in having many natural barriers in the form of mountains and seas that protected it from invasion. The borders in the lowland north, however, provided little natural protection and were open to English attack across the English Channel.

The long power struggle between the two rivals culminated in the Hundred Years' War – a series of conflicts from 1337 to 1453. At first, the war went badly for the French. Their lowest point came with the defeat at Agincourt in 1415, after which the English occupied a large part of the French king's territory, including Paris.

The French king Charles VII found a champion for France in a seventeen-year-old peasant girl. She was Joan of Arc, who claimed to have been sent by God to save her country. In 1429, Joan led the French to a brilliant victory at Orléans. However, the following year, the Burgundians captured the 'Maid of Orléans', as she was known, and handed her over to their English allies. Joan was taken to the city of Rouen, where she was put on trial, condemned as a heretic and burnt at the stake. Despite her death, the inspiration that she gave the French changed the course of the war, and the French gradually pushed the English from their country.

The Valois king Louis XII was one of France's most popular rulers. He reformed the justice system and tried to protect his people from oppression. This statue of Louis stands outside the entrance to the château at Blois, the king's favourite residence.

The symbol of French royalty was a golden fleur-de-lis (lily flower) on a blue background.

STRIFE AND UNITY

After the end of the Hundred Years' War, the Valois kings Louis XI and Louis XII were able to assert their authority over the provincial rulers. Burgundy and Provence finally became part of France. In the 16th century, however, a succession of weak kings allowed France to become involved in a disastrous civil conflict between Catholics and Huguenots. The Huguenots were French followers of Protestantism, a Christian movement that broke away from the Roman Catholic Church in the early 16th century.

In 1572, Paris was the scene of a bloodbath. During a period of truce, the Huguenot leaders came to Paris to celebrate the marriage of the king's sister, Marguerite, to the Protestant Henry of Navarre. A rumour spread that the Huguenots planned to murder the royal family. At dawn on 24 August, St Bartholomew's Day, Catholic extremists murdered the Huguenot leaders in their beds. Henry was

The national heroine

Joan of Arc is France's national heroine. Her courage and charisma helped to forge the modern French nation. She is also the country's patron saint, although the Roman Catholic Church did not make her a saint until 1920.

In times of crisis, the image of Joan of Arc has always been used as a symbol of France. During World War Two (1939–45), when France was occupied by Nazi Germany (see pages 67–8), the government in exile in London and the French collaborators both used Joan of Arc in their propaganda. When, for example, the Allies bombed Rouen, where Joan was executed, the Nazi authorities in France put out a poster depicting St Joan against the backdrop of the burning city. 'Criminals,' the poster declared, 'always return to the scene of their crime.' Even the US government used the saint's image to encourage women to join in the war effort, as in the poster above.

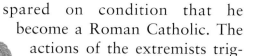

spared on condition that he become a Roman Catholic. The actions of the extremists triggered a massacre of some 3000 Huguenots in Paris, in what later became known as the St Bartholomew's Day Massacre.

In 1589, a fanatical monk assassinated the last Valois king, and Henry of Navarre became king of France. He was the first king of the Bourbon dynasty. Under the Bourbons, the **monarchy** became more and more powerful. In this period, many thinkers believed that the only way to keep the country together was by means of an all-powerful king. According to the theory of the divine right of kings, developed at about this time, the king was appointed by God and was responsible only to God. The people had to obey the king without questioning.

The Bourbon king Louis XIV, who reigned from 1643 to 1715, was the first king to put this theory into practice. He developed France into a centralized state, reorganized the army, created a navy and introduced an efficient but heavy system of taxation.

Everything centred on the king's brilliant court at Versailles, a vast palace to the south-west of Paris (see pages 44 and 95). Louis portrayed himself as the Sun King, the monarch around whom the Earth turned. The French remember the 17th century as the *grand siècle* (great century), a period when the arts flourished and France gained political dominance in Europe.

Life at the court of Louis XIV was marked by extravagant entertainments – plays, ballets and concerts – in which the king himself sometimes took part. Here he is dressed as the Sun for the ballet La Nuit *(The Night).*

Louis XIV is famous for having said 'L'État, c'est moi' ('I am the state'). He meant that he – as the king – was the all-powerful head of the French nation.

The French sometimes call the 17th and 18th centuries – before the outbreak of the French Revolution in 1789 – the *ancien régime*, meaning the 'old order'.

Under the *ancien régime*, French society was divided into three 'estates'. The First Estate was made up of the upper ranks of the clergy, the Second Estate by the nobles and the Third Estate by the people.

THE FRENCH REVOLUTION

The extravagance of the lifestyle at the palace at Versailles came to symbolize the corruption and inequalities of French life. By the 1780s, the incompetent Louis XVI had upset almost every part of French society. In May 1789, discontented members of the Third Estate – made up of the middle classes – created a National Assembly, which was determined to limit the power of the king and introduce a new **constitution**.

In the summer of 1789, resentment at the heavy taxation and a succession of poor harvests united peasants, poor city dwellers and the French middle classes in open revolt. The French Revolution had begun.

The first Bastille Day

At the heart of Paris was the fortress of the **Bastille**, which was used to hold political prisoners. The Bastille was a hated symbol

A painting made shortly after the event shows the Paris 'mob' storming the fortress of the Bastille.

PARIS DURING THE REVOLUTION

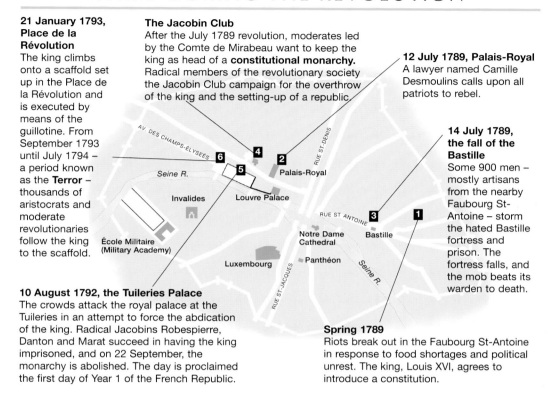

21 January 1793, Place de la Révolution
The king climbs onto a scaffold set up in the Place de la Révolution and is executed by means of the guillotine. From September 1793 until July 1794 – a period known as the **Terror** – thousands of aristocrats and moderate revolutionaries follow the king to the scaffold.

The Jacobin Club
After the July 1789 revolution, moderates led by the Comte de Mirabeau want to keep the king as head of a **constitutional monarchy.** Radical members of the revolutionary society the Jacobin Club campaign for the overthrow of the king and the setting-up of a republic.

12 July 1789, Palais-Royal
A lawyer named Camille Desmoulins calls upon all patriots to rebel.

14 July 1789, the fall of the Bastille
Some 900 men – mostly artisans from the nearby Faubourg St-Antoine – storm the hated Bastille fortress and prison. The fortress falls, and the mob beats its warden to death.

AV. DES CHAMPS-ÉLYSÉES

RUE ST-DENIS

6 **4** **2**

5

Seine R.

Palais-Royal

Invalides

Louvre Palace

RUE ST ANTOINE **3** **1**

École Militaire (Military Academy)

Notre Dame Cathedral

Bastille

Luxembourg

Panthéon

Seine R.

RUE ST-JACQUES

10 August 1792, the Tuileries Palace
The crowds attack the royal palace at the Tuileries in an attempt to force the abdication of the king. Radical Jacobins Robespierre, Danton and Marat succeed in having the king imprisoned, and on 22 September, the monarchy is abolished. The day is proclaimed the first day of Year 1 of the French Republic.

Spring 1789
Riots break out in the Faubourg St-Antoine in response to food shortages and political unrest. The king, Louis XVI, agrees to introduce a constitution.

of royal repression for many, including the *sans-culottes* ('without breeches'). These were the poor people of Paris who wore long trousers, unlike the aristocrats at court, who wore breeches and silk stockings.

In July 1789, the Paris crowds were in a black mood. There were more price rises, and the reforms promised by the king were slow in coming. On 12 July during a political meeting at a café in the Palais-Royal, a lawyer named Camille Desmoulins leapt onto a table and called the people to take up arms and fight for their liberty.

The effect was electric. The Paris crowds rose up. First, they seized weapons from the armoury at the Invalides. On 14 July, they marched on the Bastille. There its warden, the Marquis de Launay, refused to hand over the fortress, and his nervous soldiers fired on the crowd. There was a brief but fierce battle in which

Paris at the time of the French Revolution was very different from the Paris of today, with its broad boulevards and grand vistas. The city was smaller and its medieval streets were narrow and winding, making it difficult to control riots. This map shows some of the principal places and events of the revolution, with their dates.

Dr Joseph-Ignace Guillotin invented the guillotine as a more humane way of carrying out the death penalty. 'The mechanism falls,' he declared, 'like thunder; the head flies off, blood spurts, the man is no more.' The guillotine was used until 1981 when the death penalty was abolished.

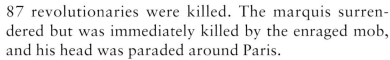

87 revolutionaries were killed. The marquis surrendered but was immediately killed by the enraged mob, and his head was paraded around Paris.

The fall of the Bastille was a turning point in the revolution – the moment when the people of Paris took matters into their own hands. It marked the symbolic birth of the French Republic, and is commemorated every year on 14 July – *la Fête Nationale* (Bastille Day).

The revolutionary cry was for '*Liberté, Égalité, Fraternité*' ('Freedom, Equality, Brotherhood'). The revolutionary government introduced for the first time many of the freedoms that we take for granted today: freedom of speech, freedom of religion and freedom from slavery. Throughout Europe, many liberals greeted the revolution with enthusiasm. The English poet William Wordsworth wrote: 'Bliss was it in that dawn to be alive.' Many kings and princes across Europe reacted with horror, concerned that the revolutionary ideas would spread to their countries. Prussia and Austria invaded France and tried to restore the old order.

The Terror

The stress of the war sent the revolution down a more radical path. By 1793, almost everyone was horrified at the nightmarish turn events had taken in Paris. The radicals, or Jacobins, among the revolutionaries – led by Maximilien Robespierre, Georges Danton and Jean-Paul Marat – gained the upper hand. The Jacobins abolished the monarchy and declared a republic. The king, Louis XVI, was executed in the Place de la Révolution (now the Place de la Concorde) in January 1793, followed in October by the queen, Marie-Antoinette.

The death of the king began the bloody period of French history known as the Terror. Thousands of royalists, moderates and other suspected anti-revolutionaries were brutally executed in front of baying crowds. The method of execution – the guillotine – was gruesome. A sharp blade dropped between two upright posts, beheading the kneeling prisoner. In the hands of such extremists as Robespierre, the guillotine became a ruthless killing machine. At the height of the Terror, 1300 heads fell in just six weeks.

One young revolutionary from Rouen named Charlotte Corday determined to put an end to the slaughter. She tricked her way into Marat's house and stabbed and killed him as he lay in a bath. At her trial, Corday declared, 'I have killed one man to save a hundred thousand.'

One Jacobin pointed out that because of the Terror, the revolution was devouring its own children. Even Danton and Robespierre eventually followed their victims to the guillotine. During the revolution, between 600,000 and 800,000 people were killed.

After Marat's death, the revolutionary government asked the celebrated painter Jacques-Louis David to paint a picture of the murdered 'Friend of the People'. The people of Paris carried the finished painting through the streets of the capital to the Louvre, where it still hangs today.

The execution of Louis XVI

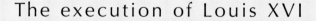

After King Louis was executed, the executioner Sanson showed the dripping head to the watching crowds. One astonished eyewitness described what happened next:

'His [the king's] blood flowed, and cries of joy from 80,000 armed men struck my ears … his blood flowed and some dipped their finger in it, or a pen or a piece of paper … An executioner [Sanson] on the boards of the scaffold sold and distributed little packets of hair and the ribbon that was used to bound them; each piece carried a little fragment of his clothes or some other bloody remnant of this tragic scene. I saw people pass by, arm in arm, laughing, chatting familiarly as if they were at a fête.'

NAPOLEON AND THE FRENCH EMPIRE

The horrors of the Terror abated after 1794 when military success and the fall of Robespierre combined to let less radical politicians take power. However, by then an anti-French alliance of Austria, Prussia, Great Britain, Holland, Sardinia and Spain was in place. Unsurprisingly, the political scene in France was also unstable.

Into this chaos stepped Napoleon Bonaparte (1769–1821). He was an army general who was born on the Mediterranean island of Corsica (see page 29). Napoleon was proclaimed First Consul of the Republic in 1799. He used the position to crush his opponents and have himself declared Consul for Life in 1802. Two years later, he was crowned Napoleon I, Emperor of the French, and declared that he would pass on the title to his descendants.

Despite this return to hereditary rule, Napoleon followed some ideas from the revolution. He abolished aristocratic privileges, established state education and reorganized the administrative and legal systems.

An English print made after Napoleon's exile to the island of St Helena shows the defeated emperor staring mournfully out to sea. For the French, however, he was a great romantic hero, as the portrait of him on page 97 shows.

Military triumphs

In addition to defending France against the hostile countries that rejected the ideas of the French Revolution, Napoleon had ambitions to create a large empire outside France, rivalling Charlemagne in his conquest of Europe. Napoleon was a brilliant military leader. Facing armies that often were far bigger than his, he would win the day by a stroke of genius, sensing when his enemies could be thrown off balance by a quick, powerful counter-attack. He earned great loyalty from his troops, who entered the battlefield under Roman-style banners decorated with Napoleon's imperial eagle.

By 1812, Napoleon controlled the greater part of central and eastern Europe. Both Austria and Prussia had been forced into alliances with France. (Prussia was a powerful country in northern Germany – at that time, a

EUROPE UNDER NAPOLEON

loose collection of numerous petty states.) Even this extensive empire did not satisfy him, however, and in that year he invaded Russia. By September, a French army of some 450,000 men and over 1000 guns had fought its way as far as Moscow. Napoleon occupied the city and waited for the Russians to surrender.

the French empire

states dependent on France

Napoleon's allies

independent states

major battles

The collapse of the French empire

By mid-October, Napoleon began to worry that his army would be cut off in Russia in winter. The French marched west again, but the Russians caught up with them as they crossed the Berezina River. Napoleon's soldiers were forced to make a hurried, shameful retreat through the bitterly cold Russian winter. Of the original

At its height in 1812, Napoleon's empire stretched well beyond the traditional borders of France, and his influence was felt throughout Europe.

450,000 men, only 25,000 survived. More defeats followed, and in 1814, a new alliance of European powers invaded France and occupied Paris. The disgraced Napoleon was exiled to the Mediterranean island of Elba.

Napoleon was not so easy to remove from power. The following year, he escaped from Elba, returned in triumph to France and formed a new army. It was all for nothing. In June, the British and Prussian allies defeated the emperor at Waterloo, in present-day Belgium, and Napoleon was sent into exile again. This time the British imprisoned him on the distant island of St Helena, where he died in 1821.

FRANCE IN THE 19TH CENTURY

From 1815 to 1830, France was ruled once again by the Bourbon dynasty of kings. In the July Revolution of 1830, the unpopular and despotic Charles X was forced into exile and replaced by a relative, Louis-Philippe. Then, in February 1848, France was rocked by a third revolution. A Second Republic was created, but it lasted only three years before being overthrown by Napoleon's nephew, Louis Napoleon, who in turn launched the Second Empire.

Known as Napoleon III, Louis Napoleon was as authoritarian as his uncle but lacked both his tactical skills and ruthlessness. He was fortunate, however, to be head of state during a period of strong economic growth. During the Second Empire, industrial production doubled, foreign trade tripled, the use of steam power increased fivefold and the length of railway tracks multiplied sixfold.

French engineering flourished, with firms building bridges, railways, docks and sewerage systems around continental Europe. One of the greatest achievements of

Napoleon's legacy

The French still remember Napoleon as one of their greatest heroes and as someone who helped to shape the modern French nation. His legacies include:
- modern French civil (non-criminal) law, which is based on the Code Napoléon
- elite schools known as *grandes écoles*
- France's highest civilian award, the **Légion d'Honneur**
- the names of many Parisian streets, bridges and railway stations. For example, the Austerlitz bridge and the Rivoli and Wagram streets all recall his military victories.

the Second Empire was the construction of the Suez Canal by engineer Ferdinand de Lesseps. By cutting through the bridge of land between Africa and Asia in Egypt, the canal linked the Mediterranean and Red seas. The sea voyage from Europe to Asia was shortened by some 7440 kilometres (4000 miles).

The Paris Commune

In 1870, Louis Napoleon was less fortunate when he launched an attack on Prussia. The French army was beaten, and the emperor taken prisoner. The Prussians laid siege to the city of Paris. The French government declared that Louis Napoleon was no longer emperor and set up a republic.

Elections were held for a new National Assembly, which agreed to the Prussian terms of surrender. Under the terms of the agreement, France would have to pay a huge compensation bill and give up the border province of Alsace and half of neighbouring Lorraine. Most humiliating of all, the Prussians were to be allowed to march through the Arc de Triomphe in Paris – a symbol of French national pride.

A group of **left-wing** radicals in Paris refused to accept the peace agreement and staged an uprising in 1871. They declared the city to be a 'commune', an area of self-rule. As the Prussians tightened their siege of the city, the communards became hungrier and hungrier. Eventually, the French national government, which was installed in Versailles, sent in troops to regain control, street by street. Some 20,000 communards were killed in the fighting or executed on the spot. Of those who survived, thousands were sent overseas to penal colonies or escaped into exile. Adolphe Thiers, the man who sent in the troops to suppress the commune, became president of the new Third Republic.

The communards of Paris make a last stand at the barricades.

The late 19th century in France saw many technological and scientific discoveries:
- **1885 – Louis Pasteur uses vaccination against rabies for the first time.**
- **1895 – The Lumière brothers develop motion pictures.**
- **1895 – Pierre and Marie Curie discover radioactivity.**

The Eiffel Tower, built in Paris in 1889 to mark the centenary (100th anniversary) of the French Revolution, was not only a great feat of engineering but also an important symbol of a country taking its place on the world stage. These photographs were taken during the construction of the tower.

THE *BELLE ÉPOQUE*

After the Franco-Prussian War, France quickly recovered. The final decades of the 19th century showed France, especially Paris, at its most brilliant and energetic. This period was later called the *belle époque* (beautiful era) by people looking back nostalgically in the 1920s.

The economy boomed as France reaped the fruits of its belated participation in the Industrial Revolution, some decades behind its rival and neighbour, Great Britain. People flocked to live and work in the cities. Huge fortunes were won and lost on the Parisian stock exchange, and people spent lavishly in the glittering shops and department stores that sprang up along the capital's new boulevards. This was the world depicted in the novels of the writer Émile Zola and in Impressionist paintings.

All over the world, people looked to Paris as the dazzling centre for social and artistic life. One critic has even called Paris 'the capital of the 19th century'. Despite the gilded image that France presented to the outside world, the country was wracked by social and economic changes. Workers were demanding more rights, women were beginning to claim equal rights with men and politicians were attacking the power of the Roman Catholic Church. There was a fierce struggle between liberals and conservatives for the upper hand in French society. Such tensions came to a head in the Dreyfus affair.

The Dreyfus affair

The brilliant *belle époque* had a dark side – anti-Semitism, or hatred of Jews. In 1894, a Jewish army officer, Captain Alfred Dreyfus (1859–1935), was accused of spying for Germany. He was condemned and imprisoned on Devil's Island in French Guiana. The case provoked a wave of anti-Semitic hysteria, despite strong evidence that Dreyfus had been wrongly accused. The Dreyfus affair divided French society. In Paris, people even fought each other in the streets over the issue. Some left-wing intellectuals, known as the *dreyfusards*, started a campaign to release Dreyfus. The novelist Émile Zola wrote a famous pamphlet 'J'accuse' ('I accuse') in support of the prisoner. It was only in 1900 that Dreyfus was pardoned and released. He was declared innocent in 1906.

THE GREAT WAR

The *belle époque* came to an end when World War One broke out in August 1914. A minor incident in the Balkans developed into war between the opposing alliances in Europe. Germany and Austria-Hungary were ranged against Britain, France and Russia. The armies fighting on the Western Front dug into a line of trenches that stretched from the English Channel to Switzerland. Over four years, despite terrible battles that cost hundreds of thousands of lives, the line barely moved (see map on page 66).

World War One was the bloodiest conflict in French history. By the time a weakened Germany agreed to an armistice (end to hostilities) in 1918, 1,325,000 French people lay dead and almost a

Lorries bring French troops to the front at Verdun, which stood close to the Belgian border. From February to December 1916, German troops assaulted the French line just north of Verdun. Although the Germans failed to take the line, the French army lost some 360,000 men in its defence.

World War One battle lines

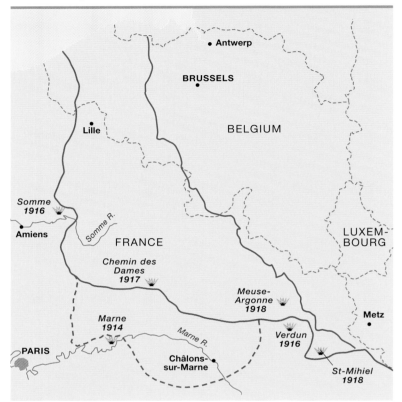

After the opening German offensive of September 1914, Allied and German troops dug in for four years of dogged trench warfare. The trenches stretched from the English Channel to the Swiss border. In the trenches, soldiers had to endure long periods of inactivity and hardship interspersed with ferocious fighting. For much of the war, despite the heavy casualties, neither side gained much land from the other. Only after 1916, when the French and British successfully held and attacked the Germans, helped by the Americans in 1917–18, did the tide begin to turn in the Allies' favour.

million more had been injured. In every town and village of France, there stands a monument dedicated to those who died in the Great War. The number of deaths had a serious effect on France's population. The economic effects were serious, too. Some experts calculate that the war cost France a quarter of its national wealth.

Disillusionment, weariness and an angry desire to make Germany pay gripped France after the war. French prime minister Georges Clemenceau rejected appeals by US president Woodrow Wilson for the victorious Allies to show generosity. In the Treaty of Versailles, signed in 1919 at Louis XIV's glittering palace to the south-west of Paris, Clemenceau took revenge on Germany not only for the Great War but also for the defeat of 1871. The terms of the treaty included the return of France's lost provinces, Alsace and Lorraine, and the reduction of Germany's armed forces. Above all, Germany was to pay France massive compensation, or reparations.

The treaty was intended to cripple Germany for good, but instead it encouraged the rise to power there of the nationalistic movement called Nazism under the leadership of Adolf Hitler. One of Hitler's aims was to revenge the humiliating terms of the Treaty of Versailles.

OCCUPATION AND RESISTANCE

Throughout the 1920s and 1930s, France tried to limit Germany's power by making alliances with other countries. Fortifications, called the Maginot Line, were built to defend France's eastern border. Nevertheless, France was eager to avoid war. Memories of the horrors of the Great War and a shortage of armaments encouraged the French government to give in to Hitler's territorial ambitions, which included reclaiming territories lost under the Treaty of Versailles, such as the Rhineland, and seizing new territories in central and eastern Europe.

In 1938, France and Britain signed an agreement in Munich, Germany, allowing Hitler to take back part of Czechoslovakia (present-day Czech Republic and Slovakia). The mood in Paris and London was one of intense relief that war had been avoided. A year later, Hitler attacked Poland, which France and Britain had pledged to defend if it was invaded by Germany. War was now inevitable.

A smiling French Resistance fighter is photographed after coming out of hiding when the Allies liberated the city of Caen, Normandy, on 9 July 1944.

France was ill prepared for war. In May 1940, the country was quickly overrun by the highly mobile German forces, and the north was placed under Nazi occupation. Further south, a puppet French state was set up. The government was based at Vichy, and its leader was a World War One military hero, Marshal Henri Philippe Pétain, who had led the troops at Verdun. The French Republic's inspiring motto of 'Liberté, Égalité, Fraternité' was replaced by a call to discipline: 'Travail, Famille, Patrie' ('Work, Family, Fatherland').

Vichy France, as the regime became known, was supposed to be independent but was in reality controlled by the Germans. Both the Vichy government and occupied France collaborated with the Nazis in deporting thousands of Jews to the death camps in Poland.

The hidden struggle

After France was occupied, many soldiers escaped to England. They formed a fighting force known as the Free French under the leadership of General Charles de Gaulle (1890–1970). To encourage the French people, de Gaulle broadcast radio messages to France via the British Broadcasting Corporation (BBC).

In German-occupied France, underground groups of patriots tried to undermine the Nazis by sending information about German military movements to London and by acts of sabotage – blowing up factories, bridges and railway tracks. Men and women of all political backgrounds took part. They were in great danger, for they could be tortured for information and shot when caught. This hidden war effort was called the Resistance because de Gaulle had made a radio broadcast in which he reminded French people of their duty to continue resistance to the occupying army.

De Gaulle returned home with the British and US forces after they landed in Normandy in June 1944. He found a country where many of the raw materials and food had been taken away by the Germans. The

General de Gaulle made his most celebrated speech from London on 18 June 1940. He called upon his fellow country men and women to rally around him. 'Whatever happens,' he said, 'the flame of the French resistance must not go out and will not go out.'

The spirit of the Resistance is summed up in this famous line from a song sung by its members: 'Friend, if you fall, a comrade will emerge from the shadows to take your place.'

68

General de Gaulle is a towering figure in the history of modern France. While many people admire him for his role during World War Two as a beacon for a future free France, some are critical of what they consider his authoritarian rule after the war.

transportation system had been severely damaged by Allied bombing and by sabotage. Thousands of homes and businesses had also been destroyed. There were 2.5 million French prisoners-of-war, conscripted (forced) workers and deportees in German camps.

After the war

The occupation left France divided between those who had worked with the Nazis and those who had resisted them. Up to 10,000 people were executed by Resistance groups as the Germans retreated. Some were killed to settle old scores rather than for collaboration.

The appearance of unity among the members of the Resistance came to an end soon after the war, as their leaders argued over a constitution for the new Fourth

'All my life I have had a certain idea about France. France is not France unless it has grandeur.' Charles de Gaulle

The war in Algeria

Algeria is a large country on Africa's Mediterranean coast and is populated mostly by Arabs. France seized the country in 1830, and many French people settled in the country, particularly in the coastal towns such as Algiers and Oran. The *pieds noirs*, or 'black feet', as Algerian-born French people are known in France, enjoyed a privileged position in Algerian society.

By the early 1950s, many Algerian people had lost patience with their French rulers. In 1954–5, the National Liberation Front (FLN) led an uprising of the Algerian people. Cafés were bombed and assassinations were committed. The French responded by pouring more than half a million troops into the country to crush the FLN. In the war that followed, the French army also committed atrocities, massacring civilians and torturing suspected FLN members.

In 1958, the crisis deepened. Extremists among the French Algerian settlers accused the French government of softening its attitude towards the Algerians. They staged a coup and threatened to declare war on France. The National Assembly panicked and turned to the retired General de Gaulle to remedy the situation. De Gaulle became French president, and began negotiations with the FLN, despite attempts on his life by an Algerian terrorist group.

The Algerian war disrupted French society as well. In Paris, Algerian immigrants grew restless. In 1961, the French police massacred between 70 and 200 Algerians taking part in a demonstration and secretly dumped their bodies into the Seine. The white French colonists, too, increasingly felt that it would be best to abandon Algeria, and in 1962 they voted in a referendum to give the colony its independence. Afterwards, the disgruntled French Algerians flooded back into France. Many eventually supported nationalistic movements that sprang up in France in the wake of colonial wars. The picture above shows FLN troops in Algiers.

Republic. De Gaulle was against the proposed draft because he said that it would lead to a weak government. When the document was narrowly approved in a referendum (national vote), he angrily withdrew from politics.

Throughout the 1950s, France was in a state of near-permanent crisis, with many changes of government. The end of the Fourth Republic came in 1958 after uprisings in two of France's colonies, Indochina (including present-day Vietnam, Cambodia and Laos) and Algeria, where armed groups were struggling for independence. It was at this desperate time that de Gaulle returned triumphantly to politics. He drafted a new constitution, and was elected first president of the new Fifth Republic.

THE FIFTH REPUBLIC

De Gaulle's constitution for the Fifth Republic is still in force today. The constitution gives strong powers to the president, who is comparatively stronger than, say, the US president. A French president is elected for seven years and can stand for re-election any number of times.

The president appoints, and can fire, the prime minister, chairs Cabinet meetings and has the right to dissolve the National Assembly. In an emergency, the

The following presidents have ruled France since the beginning of the Fifth Republic in 1959:

- C. de Gaulle (1958–69)
- G. Pompidou (1969–74)
- V. Giscard d'Estaing (1974–81)
- F. Mitterand (1981–95)
- J. Chirac (1995–)

There have been no female presidents of France.

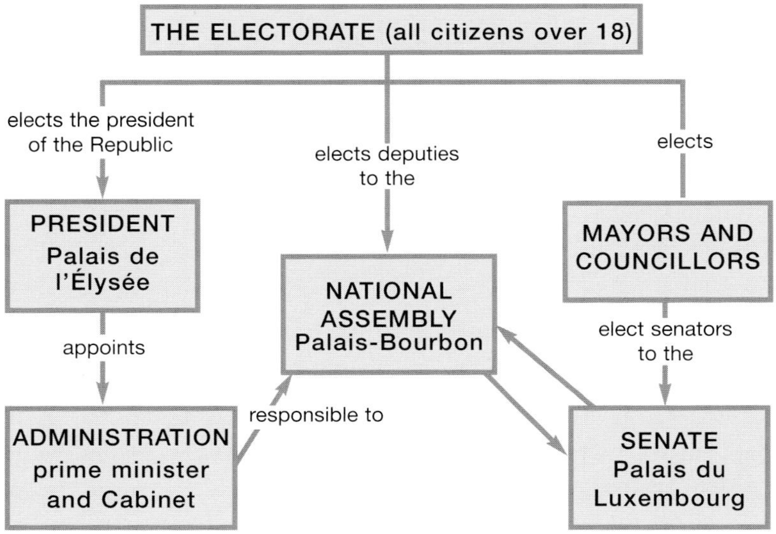

THE ELECTORATE (all citizens over 18)

elects the president of the Republic

elects deputies to the

elects

PRESIDENT
Palais de l'Élysée

appoints

NATIONAL ASSEMBLY
Palais-Bourbon

MAYORS AND COUNCILLORS

elect senators to the

responsible to

ADMINISTRATION
prime minister and Cabinet

SENATE
Palais du Luxembourg

Since the French Revolution, France has had no less than sixteen Constitutions. The constitution of the Fifth Republic, founded in 1958, increased the powers of the president and reduced those of the National Assembly. This chart shows how power works in modern France.

The prime ministers of the Fifth Republic:

- **M. Debré (1959–62)**
- **G. Pompidou (1962–8)**
- **M. Couve de Murville (1968–9)**
- **J. Chaban-Delmas (1969–72)**
- **P. Mesmer (1972–4)**
- **J. Chirac (1974–6)**
- **R. Barre (1976–81)**
- **P. Mauroy (1982–4)**
- **L. Fabius (1984–6)**
- **J. Chirac (1986–8)**
- **M. Rocard (1988–91)**
- **E. Cresson (1991–2)**
- **P. Bérégovoy (1992–3)**
- **E. Balladur (1993–5)**
- **A. Juppé (1995–7)**
- **L. Jospin (1997–2002)**
- **J.-P. Raffarin (2002–)**

president can take on special powers and is responsible for making sure that foreign treaties are upheld. This gives the president a key role in foreign policy and defence, including control of France's nuclear weapons.

The prime minister usually comes from the party or coalition of parties that has the majority in the National Assembly. The prime minister's Cabinet is appointed by the president and has the constitutional role of 'determining and directing the policy of the nation'. The roles of the president and the prime minister can overlap, particularly in matters of defence and foreign affairs. This can cause difficulties when the president and the prime minister belong to different parties. In the 1980s, for example, there was a period when a Socialist Party (left-wing) president, François Mitterrand, and a **right-wing** prime minister, Jacques Chirac, were in power together.

The French parliament has two chambers: the National Assembly and the Senate. The National Assembly is the lower chamber. It comprises 577 members who are

---

THE FRENCH PARLIAMENT IN 2002

President Jacques Chirac

National Assembly
577 members • last election 2002 • elections held every five years

UMP (Popular Movement Coalition)	62%
PS (Socialist Party)	24%
UDF (Union for French Democracy)	5%
PCF (French Communist Party)	4%
others	5%

Senate
321 members • last election 1998 • elections held every nine years

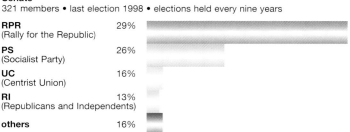

RPR (Rally for the Republic)	29%
PS (Socialist Party)	26%
UC (Centrist Union)	16%
RI (Republicans and Independents)	13%
others	16%

Regionalization: Corsica

Traditionally, France has been a highly centralized country, with the government and its powers weighted heavily towards the capital, Paris. In the last quarter of the 20th century, however, France underwent a rapid process of decentralization. A law passed in March 1982 gave much more power to the French regions (*régions*). Elected regional assemblies and their presidents gained almost complete control of local economic, social and cultural affairs.

Many people say that this development was long overdue. Particularly in areas with a strong local culture – such as Brittany, the Basque country and Corsica – many local people were dissatisfied with policies that were made in Paris and imposed with little regard for local opinion.

There are still problems. Many people of the Mediterranean island of Corsica, for example, continue to campaign for greater or even full independence from the mainland. They are proud of their history and traditions, and particularly of their language, Corsu. French road signs are frequently 'edited' with spray paint so that they give the Corsu names.

A few Corsican nationalists – people who want an independent Corsican nation – are prepared to use violence to reach their goal. The Front de Libération Nationale de la Corse (National Liberation Front of Corsica) carries out numerous bombings, bank holdups and kidnappings. In 1994, for example, there were more than 400 bombings and some 40 murders on the island. Only very few Corsicans support the terrorists, however.

elected for a five-year term. Bills put to the National Assembly and the upper chamber, the Senate, are shuttled back and forth until there is agreement. The main parties in the assembly are the Socialists (PS), the Rally for the Republic (RPR), which follows the ideas of de Gaulle, the centre-right Union for French Democracy (UDF) and the Communist Party (PCF). The president has the right to dissolve the National Assembly after consulting the prime minister and the assembly's president.

The Senate consists of 321 members elected to a nine-year term by councillors from the French departments. The Senate's main powers are to make amendments to bills and scrutinize policy-making by questioning ministers and holding investigations.

FRANCE TODAY

De Gaulle's creation has lasted well. France's politics have remained relatively stable under the Fifth Republic. The exception was an outbreak of unrest in May 1968, when students protested over proposed reforms for university education. France's stability after World War Two has been based on the wealth that was created during the first 30 years after the war and on the development of a generous health and welfare system.

The 'events' of May 1968

Not everyone was happy with de Gaulle's rule. Many young people and workers were unhappy with the government's emphasis on economic success at the expense of social reform. They also criticized de Gaulle for being too authoritarian. This student poster shows how many young people felt that the government stifled their opinions. De Gaulle in silhouette places his hand over a student's mouth – 'Be young and be quiet', the poster reads.

Dissatisfaction came to a head when, on the night of 10 May 1968, the university students of Paris set up barricades in the capital's Latin Quarter. The government responded by sending in the riot police, who brutally broke up the demonstration. Some 9 to 10 million workers came out in support of the students, and there was a national strike. France, it seemed, was on the verge of another revolution.

De Gaulle called an election, appealing to the people to support him. Many French people were frightened by 'les événements' ('the events'), as they were called, and returned de Gaulle to power by an overwhelming majority.

Nevertheless, the May 1968 'revolution' transformed French society, which became less authoritarian and more aware of social injustices. The women's, homosexual and **ecology** movements also started about this time.

Prosperity has also brought major social changes, with the arrival of immigrants from France's former colonies as well as from Portugal and Spain. In the 1950s and 1960s, immigrants were welcomed in France for taking on the boring and poorly paid jobs that the French did not want. More recently, however, they have been the target for racist and ethnic attacks, against a background of high unemployment and a depressed economy.

Another big change in recent years has been a weakening of central government in France. Some government power has been given to the 22 regional authorities in metropolitan France and to the political institutions of the European Union (EU). The European connection is important. French politicians since World War Two have focused on peace between France and what was its traditional enemy, Germany. Politicians worked to establish a lasting peace through a Treaty of Friendship.

In 1958, France and Germany joined four other countries in setting up the European Economic Community (EEC) trade area. Later this developed into the EU, with a membership of fifteen states in 2002. During the 1980s and 1990s, France and Germany were the two main countries that moved the EU towards closer integration and the transfer of some authority from national capitals to the European institutions in Brussels, Belgium, and Strasbourg, France. In January 1999, twelve EU members, including France, introduced a new single European currency, the **euro**. Local, national currencies were phased out by early 2002 (see pages 91 and 119).

The development of a united Europe has many critics, but some people argue that it is thanks to the EU that, for a whole generation of French people today, the idea of armed conflict with Germany is unthinkable.

The European Union

European Union (EU)
non-EU countries

THE NETHERLANDS
BELGIUM
GREAT BRITAIN
SWEDEN
FINLAND
DENMARK
IRELAND
GERMANY AUSTRIA
PORTUGAL
FRANCE
SPAIN
ITALY
LUXEMBOURG
GREECE

In 2002, the European Union (EU) had fifteen members. There are plans to expand membership to other European countries.

75

The economy

'The French are extremely generous both with their own wealth and that of others.'

Italian statesman Niccolò Machiavelli (1469–1527)

When people outside France think of French goods to buy, they might have in mind fashionable clothes and accessories, beauty products, perfumes and the sparkling white wine called champagne. France produces all of these, but it is also a world leader in food/agricultural production and in high-technology areas, including underground and high-speed trains, aviation and communications equipment.

An important way in which the French economy differs from other Western economies is the role of the government. In most Western countries, the government directs the economy only broadly and plays little or no role in the management of industry. In France, however, the government intervenes directly in the economy. It owns or part-owns many important industries and protects French businesses from foreign competition. This economic policy is called *dirigiste*.

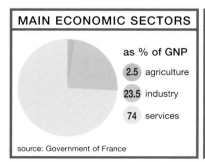

MAIN ECONOMIC SECTORS

as % of GNP

2.5 agriculture
23.5 industry
74 services

source: Government of France

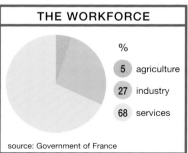

THE WORKFORCE

%

5 agriculture
27 industry
68 services

source: Government of France

The French are famous for their wines. France has some 1 million hectares (2.5 million acres) of vineyards and, after Italy, produces most of the world's wine.

ECONOMY PAST AND PRESENT

In the years before World War Two, France's strength was in agriculture – the traditional backbone of its economy. In past centuries, when times were good, France sold its food, wine and wool throughout Europe. Even when times were difficult, the country almost always had enough to feed its population. The reliance on farming and France's great size meant that industrialization came slowly. Steam locomotives, for example, began to appear in France only towards the mid-1800s, several decades after Britain and Germany.

Under the Second Empire (1852–70) and the Third Republic (1870–1940), France began to catch up with its European rivals, only to lose ground during World War One. The conflict devastated France's population growth and cost the country much of its wealth. By 1945, World War Two and occupation by Germany had cost France half a million lives and crippled its resources.

After World War Two, France remained dependent for some time on the countryside for its survival, but more and more people began to leave the land and move to towns and cities. In 1955, there were 6.1 million farmers and farmworkers. By 1995, this number had fallen to 1.5 million people.

A slow start

Up to the early 20th century, there were great differences between the levels of regional economic and industrial development within France. The country could be roughly divided by a diagonal line running from Le Havre on the north-west Atlantic coast, to Marseille on the Mediterranean in the south. The areas north and east of the line, which included Paris, had the newest and most advanced industries,

France's economy is today dominated by its trade with other members of the European Union.

MAIN TRADING PARTNERS

EXPORTS	IMPORTS

%		%	
17.1	Germany	17.4	Germany
9.3	United Kingdom	10.1	Italy
9.2	Italy	8.4	Belgium/Luxembourg
8.4	Belgium/Luxembourg	8.4	United Kingdom
7.8	Spain	7.9	USA
48.2	others	47.8	others

source: Government of France

well-developed farms and the best transportation network. Paris alone accounted for nearly one-quarter of the country's wealth and one-third of new companies chose to set up there. West and south-west of the line, only a small number of cities had any industry and agriculture was much less developed.

Today, France has more than caught up with its European neigh-bours. It has the fifth-biggest economy in the world, with a gross national product (GNP) in 2000 of 895,190 million pounds. The country is strong in most economic sectors and has a skilled workforce. The French transportation network, with excellent roads and high-speed trains, is rivalled only by Germany's. Trade is booming and the country is now the world's fourth-largest exporter.

During the 20th century, the differences in regional development across France have grown smaller. Today, the four most dynamic regions in the country are Île-de-France, Nord-Pas-de-Calais, Provence-Alpes-Côte d'Azur and Rhône-Alpes. Industry is also much more evenly distributed among the country's cities.

EXPORTS (£000 m)		IMPORTS (£000 m)	
capital goods	49.8	capital goods	43.1
consumer goods	27.8	chemicals	27.1
chemicals	27.4	consumer goods	26.9
agricultural goods	26.6	vehicles	20.3
vehicles	24.1	agricultural goods	19.9
steel and metals	15.0	steel and metals	14.6
total (including others)	181.8	energy products	13.9
		total (including others)	172.2

source: Government of France

France exports more than it imports. Like other well-developed countries with a high standard of living, France has to import a high proportion of its raw materials and energy needs.

The importance of Europe

The French often talk about 'the 30 glorious years' from 1945 to 1975 when their economy made up for its late start. In the peak period between 1958 and 1973, the French GNP doubled. The economy grew at an annual average of 5.5 per cent, higher than any industrialized country except Japan. However, after the oil crisis of the early 1970s, the French economy performed less well. The economy has continued to grow modestly over the past 25 years and many experts argue that it is now in need of a major overhaul.

Some 25,000 companies in France export products and services overseas. The top 250 of these companies account for 50 per cent of all exports.

The biggest stimulus to the economy has come from France's membership in the European Economic Community (EEC), which was the forerunner of today's European Union (EU). In 1962, this economic alliance of western European states set up a subsidy system to improve agricultural production and guarantee farmers minimum prices for their produce. Funds from the EEC were used to modernize farms, improve land yields and develop rural areas.

The biggest advantage of the EEC was that it made trading among its members easier. Before the EEC, exporters in Europe had to find their way through a maze of paperwork and customs regulations and take into account exchange rate fluctuations when they wanted to sell goods to a neighbouring country. Over the past four decades, most of these barriers have been removed and the EU, with a market of 370 million people, is now one of the world's biggest markets for trade.

France has gained a great deal from its partnership with Europe. Today, nearly half of France's trade is with its EU partners. The country's main trading partner is Germany, which is now the biggest investor in France. The economies of the two countries are today closely linked.

MAIN ECONOMIC SECTORS

The main areas of France's economy are service industries, manufacturing, agriculture and mining. Many cities such as Lille, Nantes, Strasbourg, Bordeaux and Toulouse have important industrial bases, while Paris and Lyon are also major commercial centres. The country's vast landscape of forests and fields provides France with a wealth of natural produce.

The map below shows the distribution of forest and crop and pasture land in France.

HOW FRANCE USES ITS LAND

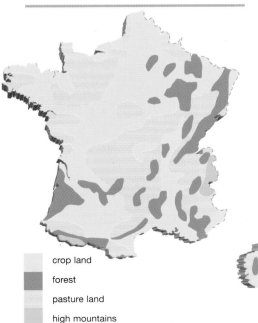

crop land

forest

pasture land

high mountains

Fields, forests and fishing

France is the world's biggest food exporter after the USA. In 1996, **exports** of food and wine accounted for a trade surplus of 6875 million pounds, more than half of the country's total trade surplus in goods of 13,125 million pounds. The biggest exports were wine and other beverages, grain, processed food, such as butter and cheese, and livestock.

Vineyards and orchards take up a lot of land. France is the biggest volume producer of wine in the world after Italy, and the country likes to boast that it also has the finest vintages (superior wines). The French government strictly regulates the quality of wine and classes it in four categories. Wine labelled *Appelation d'Origine Contrôlée* (AOC) is guaranteed to come from a well-respected wine-producing area of France and is of good quality. Some of the finest and most expensive wines in the world are made in the Bordeaux region, known for its red wine and cognac, and in the Burgundy region along the banks of the Rhône River. The area around Reims is renowned for its sparkling champagne.

The French climate is particularly favourable for growing a wealth of fruit and vegetables.

The chart below shows how France uses its land as a percentage of its total territory. Most land is given over to crops.

LAND USE

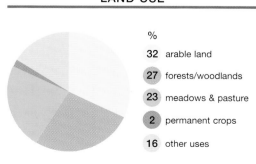

%
- **32** arable land
- **27** forests/woodlands
- **23** meadows & pasture
- **2** permanent crops
- **16** other uses

source: Government of France

Since World War Two, millions of people have left the land. Farms in France have tended to become bigger and more labour efficient – that is, they require fewer people to work them. Large food-processing corporations are getting more involved in growing crops, either by signing contracts that commit farmers to selling their harvest to the corporations or by buying the land themselves.

Forestry is another major activity in France. With more than one-quarter of its area covered by trees, France has the highest proportion of forested land in the EU – one-quarter of the EU's total forested area. Timber from these forests is used for furniture, industry and paper manufacturing. However, the country is far from self-sufficient in timber and has to import timber and timber products from Scandinavia.

Fishing is in decline, mainly because of overfishing in the Atlantic by European fleets. In recent years, there has been a move to develop fish farms to offset the decline of traditional fishing stocks. In addition to saltwater fish farms, there are freshwater farms that produce fish such as trout and salmon. Shellfish are also farmed. Oysters are harvested on the Atlantic coast, while on the Mediterranean, mussels are grown on long ropes that hang down into the water.

Minerals and energy

The land may provide plenty of food and timber, but mineral resources in France are poor. Oil and natural gas reserves are slight, accounting for less than 5 per cent of total energy needs. When oil shortages sent prices rocketing in 1973, France set up a large-scale programme to build nuclear power plants. Only able to supply 22.5 per cent of its own electricity needs in 1973, France met 51.4 per cent in 1995 thanks to inexpensive electricity generated by nuclear power. It is even able to export some electricity to the UK. But although using nuclear energy to generate electricity is inexpensive in the short term, its low cost has to be set against the enormous long-term costs of dismantling and cleaning up nuclear plants when they are taken out of service.

Coal is mined principally in the eastern region of Lorraine, but the output has fallen steadily as the coal seams become deeper and costlier to exploit. Output in 1993 was 9.07 million tonnes (8.92 million tons), compared to 48.2 million tonnes (47.4 million tons) in 1960. Apart from construction materials such as gravel, sand and calcium for cement factories, almost all important minerals have to be imported into France.

ENERGY SOURCES

%

11 oil, gas, coal and diesel

16 hydroelectricity

73 nuclear

source: Government of France

France has few natural sources of energy and today relies heavily on nuclear power to generate the large amounts of energy it needs. It still has to import some 60 per cent of its energy sources, including petroleum (from the Middle East), coal (from Germany, Australia and the USA) and natural gas (from the Netherlands, Algeria and Russia).

France has more than twenty nuclear power stations, including sites at Chinon in the Loire Valley, Gravelines in the Pas-de-Calais and Nogent on the Seine.

The Citroën 2CV, known as the Deux-Chevaux (Two Horsepower), became an endearing symbol of France in the 1950s.

The chart below shows the principal industries of France's major cities.

Manufacturing

Competition from Asian countries with low labour costs has caused France to cut back production in some industrial sectors, such as the manufacture of footwear, textiles, computers and household electrical goods. The star of French industry is the vehicle sector, which employs 300,000 people either directly in assembly plants or indirectly in vehicle parts factories and other related businesses. Output was 2100 million units in 1997, making France fourth among the world's vehicle producers. The vehicle sector enjoyed a trade surplus of some 4200 million pounds that year.

Other successful industries include aerospace companies, which build aeroplanes such as the Airbus jet and short-range jets, satellites and defence hardware. France

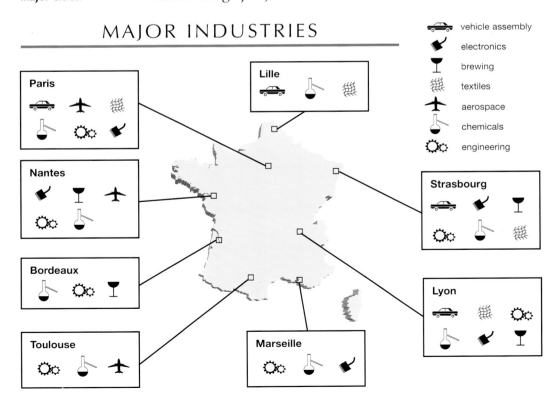

MAJOR INDUSTRIES

is the third-biggest exporter of military equipment in the world after the USA and the Russian Federation. However, sales of its most expensive goods, such as tanks and warplanes, have decreased since the fall of communism in eastern Europe in the late 1980s.

Services and tourism

The service sector of France's economy employs two-thirds of the country's working population. France has a generally unimpressive record in finance and insurance. Four French banks, however, rank among the top twenty banks in the world. France lags behind countries such as the USA and the UK in the use of personal computers.

Tourism and retailing are the largest sources of revenue in the service sector. Fifty-seven million foreigners visit France each year, the highest number of visitors to any country in the world. They provide an annual trade surplus of around 6875 million pounds. The tourist industry employs some 1.5 million people in hotels, restaurants, tourist entertainment and other related jobs.

The main tourist attractions are Paris, the beaches of the Mediterranean and the ski resorts of the Alps and the Pyrenees. There are some 20,000 **state**-approved hotels in France. These are categorized into four groups, ranging from simple one-star *auberges* (inns) to luxurious four-star hotels. For those on limited budgets, there are holiday cottages called *gîtes* (literally, 'shelters').

Nice's fine position on the sunny Côte d'Azur and its elegant hotels make this southern port one of France's most popular tourist destinations. This view shows the Promenade des Anglais (Promenade of the English), which overlooks the Baie des Anges (Bay of Angels).

MAIN FOREIGN ARRIVALS

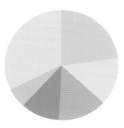

%

23 Germany

14 Belgium

14 UK

11 Italy

6 Spain

32 others

source: Government of France

France is the world's leading tourist destination. It is the most popular foreign holiday destination for the British and the Germans.

TRANSPORTATION

France's transportation system is modern, efficient and centred mainly on Paris, the capital. The country has one of the densest road networks in the world, comprising more than 810,685 kilometres (503,750 miles). Of these roads, 7041 kilometres (4375 miles) are toll motorways (*autoroutes*), connected to the road networks of neighbouring countries. These motorways make travelling across the country easy, both north to south and east to west. The latest goals are to expand the *autoroute* network to 12,970 kilometres (7500 miles) and to cut through the geological obstacles presented by the Massif Central, the Alps and the Pyrenees.

The French rail network is also highly developed, covering 32,769 kilometres (20,362 miles). The railways have undergone a revival thanks to two multibillion-pound projects: the development of the *train à grande vitesse* (TGV; high-speed train) and the building of a rail tunnel under the English Channel.

Air travel has developed greatly in France over the past few decades. International air traffic is focused primarily on the capital, Paris, which has two major airports,

The Channel Tunnel

The idea of a tunnel under the Channel linking France with England is nothing new. The French emperor Napoleon dreamed up the idea in 1802 as part of an invasion plan. The British even began to build a tunnel in 1878 but gave up after five years, having dug just 168 m (550 ft). It took the combined political powers of British prime minister Margaret Thatcher and French president François Mitterrand to complete a new tunnel in 1994.

At 50 km (30 miles), the Channel Tunnel is one of the world's longest undersea rail tunnels. By connecting England with the European continent, it is now possible to reach London from Paris by train in three hours.

TRANSPORTATION

France has one of the best transportation networks in the world. Its high-speed train links (TGV), state-of-the-art underground train systems and excellent motorways have placed it at the forefront of transportation technology.

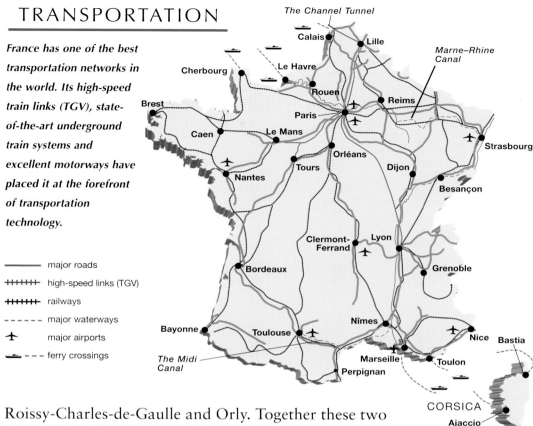

The Channel Tunnel

Calais

Lille

Marne–Rhine Canal

Cherbourg

Le Havre

Rouen

Reims

Brest

Paris

Strasbourg

Caen

Le Mans

Orléans

Dijon

Tours

Besançon

Nantes

Clermont-Ferrand

Lyon

Bordeaux

Grenoble

Bayonne

Toulouse

Nîmes

Nice

Bastia

The Midi Canal

Marseille

Toulon

Perpignan

CORSICA

Ajaccio

——— major roads

+++++ high-speed links (TGV)

+++++ railways

- - - - major waterways

✈ major airports

⛴ - - - ferry crossings

Roissy-Charles-de-Gaulle and Orly. Together these two airports handle some 80 million passengers every year. Other city airports such as those in Lille, Strasbourg, Nice and Marseille are used for short-haul routes to neighbouring countries. The national airline is Air France.

For many years, domestic flights in France were expensive as only the government could operate them. Now that the government monopoly has ended, ticket prices are lower as airlines are competing for passengers.

The other main form of transportation in France is barge. The Rhine, Rhône and Seine rivers, and a canal system in northern and eastern France, are important waterways. The traffic on these waterways increased enormously during the second half of the 20th century. To meet this growing demand, the French government has undertaken a massive improvement and expansion of the nation's canal system.

Important waterways in France include:

• **the Marne-Rhine, linking Paris with Strasbourg**

• **the recently completed Rhine–Rhône, linking the North Sea with the Mediterranean**

Getting places fast

The French national train company, the Société National des Chemins de Fer (SNCF), was founded in 1937. It was largely state owned and was quickly able to build up one of the best train networks in the world. One of SNCF's major innovations has been the introduction, in 1981, of a high-speed train, or TGV (*train à grande vitesse*).

In its rivalry with Japan's bullet train for the world's speed crown, the TGV has notched up a record 515 km/h (320 mph). On scheduled journeys, it cruises at up to 301 km/h (187 mph). The train has to run on a specially built electrified track and its carriages have to be insulated to absorb the shockwave caused by entering a tunnel at high speed. At present, there are TGVs in operation between Paris and Lyon, Paris and Calais via Lille and Paris and Le Mans and Tours.

TGV trains stand in Montparnasse station in Paris. These high-speed trains make travelling between some of France's major cities quick and easy.

THE ROLE OF THE STATE

A central feature of the French economy is the important role played by the state (government). Since the early 1980s, many Western governments have tended to loosen the reins on their economies, and instead they have left it up to private individuals and companies to create wealth and provide employment. Nationally owned industries have been sold into private hands and citizens are increasingly expected to provide for themselves. France has gone against this trend almost alone.

Today, the French state continues to be the biggest producer, the biggest customer and the biggest employer in the country. The government employs more than 2 million people, who benefit from early retirement and long paid holidays. The state is also the biggest transporter, the biggest owner of land and property and the biggest distributor of energy. It has modernized France's transportation network and its electricity and gas supplies and has carved out a role for the country in high-technology industries, such as aircraft building and aerospace development.

The state's grip on the economy was strengthened by the wave of nationalizations carried out by the socialist government in 1981. (An industry or business is said to be nationalized when it is brought under state control.) One-quarter of industry and 90 per cent of all bank deposits were brought under state control. Some very large companies, such as the airline Air France, the steel giant Usinor-Sacilor, the bank Crédit Lyonnais and the computer firm Bull, ran into problems and survived only because of government subsidies (financial support) worth millions of pounds. Several of the nationalizations have since been reversed, or sometimes the government has sold a minority stake in a business to the public. Most, however, remain in state hands.

Arguments for and against

Supporters of the state's strong role in the economy say that there are cases when only the government is able to put money and effort into long-term projects such as the TGV. They argue that the state can also give stability to important companies that run into difficulties and can provide finance to those developing new products.

Critics of state intervention say the government should have no role in business and argue that the state's support is unhelpful. Many argue that poorly managed companies that receive large government subsidies do not make enough effort to improve their performance,

Nationalized and part-nationalized French industries include:
• postal and telecommunication services (Postes et Télécommunications)
• electricity (Électricité de France)
• gas (Gaz de France)
• coal (Charbonnages de France)
• transportation (notably the national rail company, SNCF)
• many banks
• armaments

The fashion industry

France is a renowned exporter of luxury consumer products, including clothes, perfumes, jewellery and cosmetics. The *haute couture* (dress design) of Paris's top fashion houses, such as Cartier, Yves Saint Laurent, Christian Dior and Chanel, are widely admired and much copied. The Paris fashion shows, held twice a year, are high-profile events that display France at its best – a country of grace and creativity that can be fresh and often brilliant.

Despite the glamour of such events, the French clothing industry is today in decline in the face of strong foreign competition. The perfume and cosmetics industries alone remain world leaders. The elegant perfume bottle below contains *L'Air du temps* – one of the most expensive scents in the world.

as they come to depend on the government to assist them when they are in difficulties. Critics also maintain that the government's repeated assistance for badly run companies has stifled initiative in the private sector. France is especially lacking in business pioneers and entrepreneurs.

Public and private

In the private sector, there are a high number of medium- and small-sized companies. Few French companies are as large as the giant US, British and German corporations. In 1997, only nine French corporations, many of them run by the government, are listed among the world's 100 biggest companies.

Among the stars of industry are two rival vehicle manufacturers of roughly equal size, Renault and PSA, which make the Citroën (see page 84) and Peugeot brands, and the vehicle components company Valeo.

In the pharmaceutical industry, Rhône-Poulenc and Roussel-Uclaf have succeeded both at home and overseas, as have the petrochemicals groups Elf-Aquitaine and Total. Other very successful

French firms include the construction company Bouygues, the services group Vivendi, the huge energy and telecommunications corporation Alcatel and the dairy products group Danone – France's biggest corporation in the food-processing sector.

THE NEED FOR CHANGE

During the '30 glorious years', French governments were good at keeping their budgets under control. The **national debt** surged, however, after the Socialist Party came to power in 1981 and bought up dozens of industrial corporations and banks. The government's debts increased in the 1990s as the cost of the welfare system became higher, particularly as unemployment increased. Part of government spending was covered by increases in taxation and the rest by borrowing.

The result is that the private sector has been badly affected by the cost of taxation. Sales tax, profits tax and payroll costs in France are among the highest in advanced industrialized countries. Employment conditions are also tightly regulated and the legal working week, at 35 hours, is one of the shortest in the world. Many companies have been forced into liquidation or have had to move their businesses abroad, notably to eastern Europe, increasing unemployment.

Some people argue that in order to break this vicious circle, the government must reform the welfare system and cut back the government-owned sector. Such reforms, however, run counter to the high expectations of the French public who expect the state to help them.

It will require a firm and clever government, or a deep crisis, to change this way of thinking. Most of the people in power in France are hesitant about taking the tough option. Instead, they look to the single European currency – the **euro** (see pages 75 and 119) – as a means of giving the French economy a boost.

Some famous logos from French businesses (from top to bottom): the state-owned national airline Air France, the giant pharmaceutical corporation Rhône-Poulenc and the privately owned vehicle company Peugeot-Citroën.

The national debt in 1996 was 469,000 million pounds, equivalent to 55.5 per cent of the GNP, compared with 344,000 million pounds and 34.2 per cent just three years earlier.

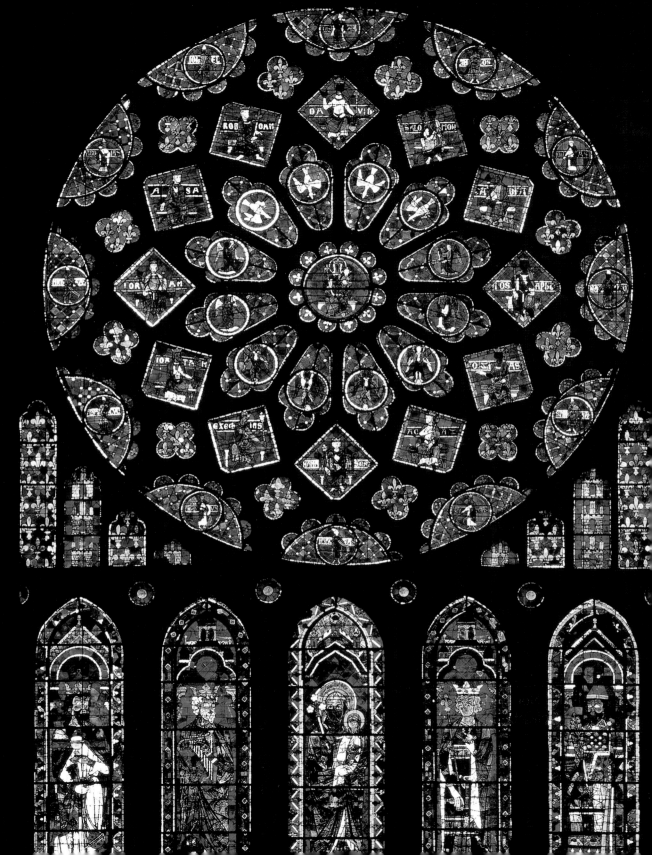

Arts and living

'In France everyone seems to have wit and intelligence.'

French writer S.-R. N. Chamfort (1740–94)

The French are very proud of their culture and way of life. Their country's beautiful art and architecture, the finesse of its cookery and its innovative films are known throughout the world. For many people, the traditional French lifestyle is associated with ease and style.

Today, some of these traditions are dying. For example, cafés where people once lingered over carefully cooked meals are closing down, while fast-food restaurants are opening up. On the other hand, in recent years, France has been enriched by the culture of its immigrant communities. For example, French popular music has been influenced by the energetic rhythms of North Africa.

ART AND LITERATURE

France has produced some of the world's finest writers, philosophers and artists, as well as some of its most imaginative film directors. In the past, many artists and writers from other countries came to Paris because it was a centre of artistic activity.

Running through French culture are two opposing traditions that play against each other. On the one hand, there is a commitment to the human rights and ideals set out in the French Revolution slogan, '*Liberté, Égalité, Fraternité*' ('Freedom, Equality, Brotherhood'). This has led many artists to be willing to experiment and to challenge old ideas. This tradition is sometimes called the

The Gothic cathedrals of the Middle Ages often had magnificent stained-glass windows. This rose window at Chartres measures 9 metres (14 feet) in diameter.

romantic spirit. On the other hand, there is a **conservative** tradition in France that stems from the influence of the Roman Catholic Church. This tradition – sometimes called the classical tradition – values authority and order and has a strong respect for the past.

A grand tradition of architecture

The most ancient structures in France are the simple but impressive monuments erected by the Neolithic farmers and herders of Brittany some 4000 to 5000 years ago. These include huge standing stones called menhirs (Breton for 'long stone') and stone burial chambers called dolmens. The latter are sometimes buried deep beneath an artificial mound of earth called a tumulus and reached by a long, narrow passage. Menhirs sometimes form stone circles or long lines called *alignements* that stretch across the moorlands of upland Brittany.

The first great age of architecture in France was during the 12th and 13th centuries, when the Gothic cathedrals were built. Architects, engineers, masons and sculptors worked together over many years to produce these huge, awe-inspiring buildings. The beautiful cathedral at Chartres, for example, took 25 years to build – a relatively short amount of time by the standards of the period. There are Gothic cathedrals at Reims, Amiens and at many other cities across France.

The Gothic cathedrals, which were first built in northern France, often feature soaring spires, pointed arches, slender columns, ribbed vaulted ceilings and numerous richly coloured stained-glass windows. Sometimes the stained glass took the form of a vast rose (circular) window. Chartres has more than 160 windows, including three spectacular rose windows.

Standing stones are sometimes called megaliths, meaning simply 'big stones'.

Below is a plan of a Gothic cathedral. Many French cathedrals were oriented roughly east to west so that the altar in the chancel faced towards the city of Jerusalem. However, this meant that the altar faced away from the congregation. This arrangement has recently changed.

belfry (bell tower)
columns
sacristy
porch
nave
transept
chancel
transept
south tower
N
chapels

Because of the amount of glass used in the walls of the cathedral, engineers had to add bulky stone buttresses to the outside in order to carry the weight of the roof. The dizzying sensation of space and light created inside a cathedral still inspires awe and wonder.

From the 16th century on, French kings and aristocrats vied with each other to build the finest and grandest **châteaus**. These were designed as elegant country residences rather than strongholds. The most lavish château of all was at Versailles, built for the 'Sun King', Louis XIV. The dazzling Hall of Mirrors in the palace is 37 metres (120 feet) long and lit by seventeen windows, facing which are numerous mirrors that reflect back the light.

After the French Revolution, the French continued to construct buildings that were designed to impress or to show off their country's greatness. Under the French emperor Napoleon, Paris gained some of its most famous sights, including the grandiose Arc de Triomphe and the rather classical church of La Madeleine.

At the end of the 19th century, the Eiffel Tower (see page 41), made up of iron latticework, was, at 300 metres (984 feet) high, the world's tallest structure. In this period, many buildings were built in the art nouveau (new art) style. Underground stations, shops and hotels were made from glass, iron and brick, and decorated with flowing lines and natural forms such as water lilies and insect wings.

The 17th-century palace of Versailles is surrounded by vast gardens laid out with fountains, statues and formal flower beds.

More than 22,000 workers laboured half a century to build Versailles. This vast palace could house 1000 courtiers and 4000 servants.

Versailles was the site of the signing of the 1919 treaty between the Allies and Germany that brought World War One to a close.

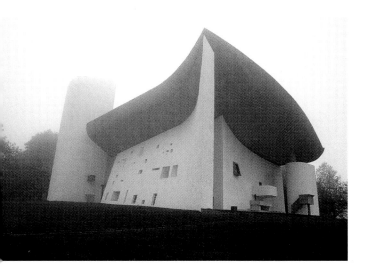

In the 20th century, France continued to pioneer innovative and striking architecture. The Swiss-born Le Corbusier (1887–1965) built almost all of his most famous buildings in France. He made his concrete villas and apartment blocks out of simple forms such as the cube and sphere. One of his famous comments was that a house was simply 'a machine for living'.

One of Le Corbusier's most striking and beautiful buildings is this chapel, built in 1955 at Ronchamp in eastern France.

Many 20th-century French presidents, like King Louis XIV before them, built grand public buildings that would help ensure their place in history. Such buildings are often called *grands projets* (grand projects). Georges Pompidou built the colourful Centre Beaubourg, also known as the Centre Pompidou, the upper levels of which contain an important collection of modern art. Giscard d'Estaing began the transformation of a derelict railway station in Paris into the Musée d'Orsay, a huge museum of 19th-century art, while President François Mitterrand commissioned a whole series of daring buildings (see page 44).

The art of painting

From the 18th century to the early 20th, French painters led the way in introducing new styles and subject matter to their paintings. Rich collections of their art can be found in the Louvre and the Musée d'Orsay in Paris, as well as in numerous *musées des beaux-arts*, or fine-art museums, in provincial capitals such as Lille.

The first paintings in France were the vivid bulls and wild horses painted on the walls of caves at Lascaux, close to the Dordogne River, some 17,000 years ago (see pages 49 and 50). However, the history of French painting really begins in the Middle Ages when artists

French painters and sculptors traditionally showed their paintings at public art exhibitions called *salons*. Artists submitted their work to a jury, who decided whether it was good enough to be shown.

produced decorated prayer books for their rich and pious patrons. These miniature paintings showed scenes from ordinary life – tending a vineyard or taking in the harvest – and were painted in bright, jewel-like colours.

The first great painter in France was Nicolas Poussin (1594–1665). Poussin spent much of his life in Rome and produced carefully crafted landscapes and scenes from Greek and Roman mythology. In the 18th century, painting was mostly in the graceful, even light-hearted style called rococo. François Boucher (1703–70) produced not only paintings but also tapestries in this style for the pleasure-loving aristocracy, while Antoine Watteau (1684–1721) painted wistful pictures of departing lovers and lonesome clowns. Jean-Baptiste Chardin (1699–1779) worked in a more sober style, producing some of the greatest still lifes – pictures of objects such as fruit and flowers – ever painted.

During the French Revolution, Jacques-Louis David painted grand historical scenes with clear republican messages. His most famous painting is *The Death of Marat* (see page 59). David later became court painter to the French emperor Napoleon.

In the early 19th century, a new movement in painting arose – Romanticism. The new artists produced paintings that were full of passion and energy. The huge canvases of Eugène Delacroix (1798–1863), with their rich colours and swirling compositions, depicted dramatic scenes from history or exotic scenes from the French colonies.

In the mid-19th century, a new generation of artists rebelled against the excesses of the Romantics. They aimed to depict life and nature as it really was, preferring landscapes and everyday scenes to historical or

Jacques-Louis David painted this striking portrait of French emperor Napoleon on horseback in 1801. Napoleon is shown at the Great St Bernard Pass in the Alps, before his victory at the Battle of Marengo in 1800.

The Impressionists

The Impressionists have left a remarkable record of late 19th-century France, with fresh and colourful scenes of young Parisian couples walking in the park, boats on the Seine, young dancers rehearsing a ballet, the countryside beyond the city walls or the changing effects of light on a cathedral.

Often working outdoors (*en plein air*), the Impressionists tried to record landscapes and other scenes spontaneously. They used bright, contrasting colours and emphasized individual brushstrokes to represent the natural effect of light. The new technique shocked people because it was so different from the conventional art of the period, which often featured traditional themes from the Bible, mythology and history.

The critic Louis Leroy, who first used the term 'impressionist', meant it as an insult. On seeing Monet's 1874 work *Impression, soleil levant* (*Impression, sunrise*), he suggested that Monet should have looked a little longer before he started painting!

At first, the Impressionists were refused admission to the main art exhibitions in Paris and had to put on a series of independent shows in order to show the public their work. Most Impressionist artists lived in great poverty, selling their work for money to buy

Claude Monet ©ADAGP, Paris and DACS, London 1999

Claude Monet, **La Rue Montorgeuil, à Paris: Fête du 30 Juin, 1878**

food and paint. Today, however, their paintings are sold for record prices. Claude Monet's beautiful garden at Giverny in Normandy, where he painted his famous pictures of water lilies, has become a place of pilgrimage for art lovers from around the world.

The painting above depicts a street festival in Paris and was painted by Monet in 1878.

mythological subjects. The new art movement was called **Realism**. Gustave Courbet (1819–77) was the greatest Realist painter. Until Courbet, everyday life was shown only in small paintings – large canvases were for 'important' subjects, such as scenes from the Bible or history. Courbet was one of the first artists to paint ordinary scenes such as a funeral or even his own studio on a grand scale. The huge *Burial at Ornans*, for example, measures 315 by 668 centimetres (124 by 263 inches).

The search for truth in painting gave birth to another new movement – Impressionism (see box opposite). Influenced by Edouard Manet (1832–83), the artists who originated the movement included Claude Monet (1840–1926), Pierre-Auguste Renoir (1841–1919) and Berthe Morisot (1841–95). Edgar Degas (1834–1917) also had important links to the Impressionists.

In the wake of Impressionism, younger artists continued to experiment still further with colour and paint. Paul Gauguin (1848–1903) painted pictures of the French colony of Tahiti in Polynesia, using bright colours and flat, simplified forms. Paul Cézanne (1839–1906) painted scenes and people from the south of France. He wanted to bring a sense of order and solidity to the experiments of the Impressionists. To do so, he looked back to the classical landscapes of Poussin, which taught him to see in nature the fundamental shapes of the cylinder, sphere and cone.

Cézanne in turn inspired Georges Braque (1892–1963) and the Spanish-born Pablo Picasso (1881–1973), who together devised Cubism. In their work, these artists tried to show a subject – a guitar, a person or bottle of wine – from several points of view at once. Sometimes they used collages to enrich the viewer's sense of the object depicted. They made pictures by sticking pieces of newspaper, string or wood onto the canvas.

The work of Henri Matisse (1869–1954), Raoul Dufy (1888–1964) and their friends was more sensuous. They portrayed the light-flooded landscapes of

The Musée d'Orsay in Paris is the most important place to see the paintings of the Impressionists. There are, however, many good Impressionist collections in Britain.

southern France in bold, bright colours that often had no relation to reality. Their paintings caused such a shock when critics first saw them that the artists were nicknamed *les fauves* (the wild beasts).

Tapestry and one so-called tapestry

During the Middle Ages, the French became expert tapestry-makers. Tapestries are colourful, woven hangings that were originally designed to cover bare walls in the houses of the rich. In the Middle Ages, a lord often had no fixed home but travelled from place to place to oversee his properties. He had to carry most of his furniture and furnishings with him, so these needed to be portable. A tapestry could be easily rolled up and carried, and it also helped to keep draughty castle rooms warm.

Northern French towns such as Paris, Arras and Tournai were important centres for tapestry production. The tapestries often showed hunting scenes, gardens or scenes from popular stories. These pictures were often full of vivid details, including animals such as rabbits and hares and a profusion of jewel-like flowers. One style of tapestry included so many flowers that it was called *mille fleurs*, meaning 'a thousand flowers'.

The most famous tapestry in France is not, strictly speaking, a tapestry at all. The Bayeux Tapestry shows the invasion of England by Norman duke William the Conqueror in 1066 (see page 51) and dates from shortly after. Rather than being woven, it is a 73-metre-long (240-foot) strip of linen embroidered with a few coloured wools.

According to French tradition, William's wife, Matilda, made the tapestry with her court women, and the French call it the 'Tapestry of Queen Matilda'. Today, the tapestry is

In this scene from the Bayeux Tapestry, William, Duke of Normandy, encounters Harold, the king of England. Along the borders of the tapestry are strange animals and mythical beasts.

displayed in a museum in Bayeux in Normandy, from which it gets its English name. The Bayeux Tapestry is like a comic strip, recording in words and pictures the events leading up to the conquest. Besides being an important historical document, the tapestry gives a vivid picture of the life of medieval soldiers.

In the 17th century, the kings of France held a virtual monopoly over tapestry production. Most tapestries were made at the royal Gobelins factory in Paris.

Literature and thought

The literature of France has a long and rich history, and the novels, poems and plays written by the French over the centuries are among the classics of world literature. France's very oldest piece of writing is the 11th-century epic *La Chanson de Roland* (*The Song of Roland*). This recounts the death of Roland, the nephew of the Frankish emperor Charlemagne (see pages 48 and 51), who is ambushed on his return from fighting the Muslims in Spain in 778.

The first great age of French literature was the 17th century. Under the patronage of King Louis XIV and his ministers, Pierre Corneille, Jean Racine and Jean-Baptiste Molière wrote plays in verse, many for performance at court. The plays of Corneille and Racine were tragedies in a strict classical style. Molière wrote witty and entertaining comedies, such as *Tartuffe* and *The Misanthrope*, in which he made fun of society.

This portrait of the French writer Voltaire shows him in old age.

In the 18th century, some great writers were deeply critical of the poverty and inequalities of life under the aristocracy (see page 55). The playwright Pierre Caron de Beaumarchais (1732–99) is best remembered for his character of Figaro, a smart, witty barber who exposes the dullness and stupidity of the count who employs him. A contemporary of Beaumarchais was Voltaire (the

A poem by Victor Hugo

The French poet and novelist Victor Hugo led a very dramatic life. One of its most tragic episodes occurred in Normandy in 1843, when his beloved daughter Léopoldine drowned with her husband while boating on the Seine. Hugo meditated for many years on his daughter's death and on his own grief. This is one of many poems he wrote on the subject.

Tomorrow, at dawn, when the landscape
*   turns white*
I will set out. I know that you are waiting
*   for me.*
I will go by the forest, I will go by the
*   mountain.*
No longer can I remain apart from you.

I will walk with eyes fixed on my thoughts.
I will see or hear nothing of the world outside.
I will be alone, a stranger, with my back bent
*   and my hands crossed.*
I will be sad. Day will be for me like night.

I will not look at the golden fall of evening
Nor at the distant sails going down to Harfleur.
And when I arrive, I will place on your tomb
A bouquet of green holly and flowering
*   heather.*

pen name of François-Marie Arouet). Voltaire was a prolific writer who spent much of his life in exile for his biting attacks on tyrants everywhere. In his short novel *Candide*, he attacked intolerance and questioned whether God could be either good or just when people suffer earthquakes, torture and disease.

As an art form, the novel came into its own in the 19th century. Honoré de Balzac (1799–1850) and Émile Zola (1840–1902) both wrote long series of novels that set out to depict every aspect of French society. Unlike Zola and Balzac, Gustave Flaubert (1821–80) wrote very few books. He was a perfectionist, painstakingly reworking each sentence he wrote until he was happy with it. Flaubert's most famous novel is *Madame Bovary*, the story of the wife of a provincial doctor who yearns for a more romantic life in Paris.

Victor Hugo (1802–85) is a giant of 19th-century French literature, whose career as a novelist, playwright and poet spanned much of the century. His early work, including two collections of poetry and the novel *Notre Dame de Paris* (*The Hunchback of Notre Dame*), was greatly influenced by the Romantics. The novel is an exciting adventure story, with colourful characters such as the hunchback Quasimodo and the exotic gypsy girl Esmeralda. Later, Hugo's opposition to the emperor Napoleon III forced him into exile on the island of Jersey, in the English Channel, where he wrote his famous novel *Les Misérables*. The novel is a powerful attack on social injustice. After Hugo's death in 1885, more than 2 million people followed his funeral procession through Paris.

The 20th century produced a wealth of poets, novelists and playwrights. Many worked in highly experimental styles. At the beginning of the century, Marcel Proust (1871–1922) wrote the seven-volume novel *À la recherche du temps perdu* (*In Search of Lost Time*). The novel is famous for its long sentences that sometimes last a page or more, but it is also a brilliant portrayal of society during the *belle époque* (see pages 64–5).

A major intellectual movement called **Existentialism** emerged in France after World War Two. Its followers believed that because life essentially had no meaning, it was up to individuals to shape their own lives through their actions. Important figures in this movement were the writers Simone de Beauvoir (1908–86) and Jean-Paul Sartre (1905–80). Sartre and de Beauvoir were lifelong companions, and after World War Two, were often to be found in the cafés of the Latin Quarter in Paris.

Both writers believed in the importance of being committed to a cause to give meaning to life. While Sartre mainly produced lengthy philosophical works that developed Existentialist ideas, de Beauvoir wrote studies that examined and sought to change contemporary society. Her most famous work is *The Second Sex* (1949), a massive study of women and their position in society. In this book, she famously stated that 'women are made and not born', meaning

> Since 1904, the prestigious Prix Goncourt is awarded yearly to the best new French novel.

French thinker Simone de Beauvoir wrote novels, plays and philosophical works, as well as a series of moving and revealing autobiographies. Her feminism and her passionate life still inspire many men and women today.

that women are brought up to behave in a 'feminine' way and have the choice to change their behaviour. De Beauvoir's book was a major influence on the feminist movement.

By contrast with the Existentialists, younger writers such as Nathalie Sarraute and Boris Vian developed the *nouveau roman* (new novel), which abandoned traditional conventions of the novel, such as plot and identifiable characters. Today, the *nouveau roman* has become unpopular, and more traditional forms of storytelling are re-emerging.

The French are enthusiastic readers. Every year some 30,000 titles are published in France, of which nearly half are new works. Comic books, called *bandes dessinées*, are also very popular. Overseas, the most famous of these are the adventures of Astérix, a Gaulish warrior who resists the Roman occupiers of France (see page 50).

The birthplace of film

France is the birthplace of motion pictures. Two brothers, Auguste and Louis Lumière, developed the first film projector, the *cinématographe*, and also held the first public film screening at the Grand Café in Paris in 1895. This film showed workers leaving the Lumière brothers' photography factory.

In the 1920s and 1930s, filmmakers such as Jean Renoir (1894–1979), son of the great Impressionist artist Auguste Renoir, and Abel Gance (1889–1981) experimented boldly with the new medium. Gance, for example, made a four-and-a-half-hour-long epic about

The most famous New Wave film is Au bout du souffle *(Breathless), directed by Jean-Luc Godard in 1960. The film centres on a love affair between a young American in Paris, played by US actress Jean Seberg (left), and a doomed gangster, played by French star Jean-Paul Belmondo (right).*

French emperor Napoleon (1927), while Renoir made satirical films that gently mocked contemporary society. His *Boudu Saved from Drowning* (1932) is the story of a Parisian tramp who, saved from a suicide attempt in the river Seine, goes to live in the home of his rescuer, a middle-class bookseller.

In the 1950s, a group of young filmmakers began to make fresh, lively films that broke away from traditional French cinema. The new style of cinema, called the **Nouvelle Vague**, or New Wave, used groundbreaking techniques, such as jump cuts and improvised dialogue, and avoided the lavish studio sets that were the norm for traditional French films. New Wave filmmakers included Jean-Luc Godard and François Truffaut.

In the second half of the 20th century, cinema faced stiff competition from television. Nevertheless, French cinema is still vibrant. France has the third-biggest film industry in the world, after the USA and India. The government supports the industry generously with tax concessions and grants. Every year, the beach resort of Cannes hosts the most prestigious film festival in the world. Directors everywhere covet the festival's main prize, the Palme d'Or (Golden Palm).

> The French go to the cinema far less than they used to. During the 1950s, some 450 million seats were sold per year. Today, the figure is only about 120 million.

French *chanson*

French traditional song is called *chanson*, meaning simply 'song'.

Chanson has its origins in the Middle Ages, when troubadours roamed the south of France singing songs about love, war and politics. The French national anthem, 'La Marseillaise', is rooted in this tradition. *Chanson* was revived in the 1930s by singers such as Edith Piaf (real name Edith Gassion, 1915–1963), Maurice Chevalier and Georges Brassens. Piaf (right) was famous for her deep, husky voice and tiny physique. Her stage name 'Piaf' means 'sparrow' in Parisian slang.

EVERYDAY LIFE

One of France's proudest achievements is its pleasant lifestyle and *joie de vivre* (joy of living). Delicious food, good clothes and long holidays at the beach or on the ski slopes are considered almost a right in France. People often talk about *qualité de vie* (quality of life) as a way of measuring whether things are good or bad.

Many French towns have busy markets where fresh, local produce is temptingly on display. The French are very discerning and expect to be able to touch and smell the fruits and vegetables before they buy.

Food and drink

Food lies at the heart of the French way of life. Good cooking has been a French tradition for centuries, and the kitchen remains the centre of the household. When people go to the cinema or for a walk, the day often ends with a three-course meal at a restaurant or at someone's house. Weddings, particularly in the countryside, are marathon events where people sit down at the table after noon and are unlikely to go home before midnight!

Even the smallest dish or snack is served with flair. A simple radish is often given a dab of Normandy butter to enhance the flavour, and a tiny gherkin (sweet pickle)

How to make tarte Tatin

An upside-down apple pie, thrown together in a rush by a distracted chef in 1898, is one of France's best-known dishes. The tarte Tatin was created when two sisters, Stéphanie and Caroline Tatin, forgot to make desserts for customers at their hotel in Lamotte-Beuvron, in the north-western region of Sologne. One of the sisters went into the kitchen, found some peeled apples, tossed them into a pan, added butter and sugar and left them to cook on the stove. Distracted by a client, she forgot about the pan and returned to the kitchen some time later to find that the apples had a caramelized coating. The hurried cook covered the unusual mixture with pastry and placed the pie in the oven to bake. When she took the tart out of the oven, she was horrified by the pastry's rough appearance and decided to turn the pie upside down on a platter. The tarte Tatin was born!

Serves four to six people

For the pastry:
110 g (4 oz) plain flour
pinch of salt
50 g (2 oz) butter
cold water

Sift the flour and salt into a large mixing bowl. Cut the butter into small cubes and add them to the flour. Then gently rub together between your fingers until the mixture is crumbly. Add a little cold water until you have a smooth ball of dough. Wrap it in foil or plastic wrap and leave it in the refrigerator for 20–30 minutes.

For the apples:
6 large sweet apples
110 g (4 oz) butter
2 or 3 tablespoons of sugar

Peel and core the apples and cut them into neat, thick slices. Place them in a frying pan with the butter and sugar, and cook gently until a thick caramel forms. This takes about half an hour. Arrange the apples in a buttered 20 cm (8 in) dish. Roll out a circle of pastry and cover the apples with it.

   Bake in a hot oven at 180 °C (350 °F) for 25 minutes. Turn upside down on a plate and serve very hot with ice cream or cream.

HOW THE FRENCH SPEND THEIR MONEY

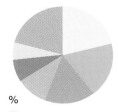

%

21.3 housing

18.3 food/drink/tobacco

16.4 transport/communications

10.2 health/medicine

7.4 entertainment/sports

5.7 clothing

20.7 other

source: Government of France

Here are just some of France's reputed 365 cheeses.

may be added to a slice of garlic sausage to add a crunchy texture. At the other end of the scale are elaborate dishes that can take two days to prepare and are enjoyed with vintage wine. Especially prized are Perigord truffles. This wild fungus grows underground in south-western France and is sniffed out by trained pigs or dogs. Truffles can cost their weight in gold because of the unique flavour they give to omelettes and desserts.

Every part of France has its own wine and ham, and the French like to boast that they have 365 cheeses – one for each day of the year. Among them are goat's cheeses rolled in the ashes of burnt leaves to give a special flavour and cheeses made from sheep's milk. Camembert and Brie, soft and creamy and covered with a rind, have been copied in many countries.

Bread usually accompanies a meal, and there are many kinds. The French stick, called the baguette, and the croissant, the breakfast pastry named after the crescent moon, are found everywhere in France. For special occasions, there are delicious *pains au chocolat* (chocolate croissants) and almond pastries.

Food and drink

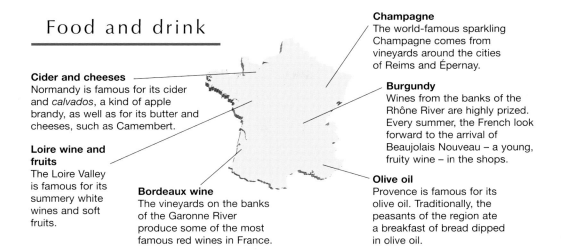

Champagne
The world-famous sparkling Champagne comes from vineyards around the cities of Reims and Épernay.

Cider and cheeses
Normandy is famous for its cider and *calvados*, a kind of apple brandy, as well as for its butter and cheeses, such as Camembert.

Burgundy
Wines from the banks of the Rhône River are highly prized. Every summer, the French look forward to the arrival of Beaujolais Nouveau – a young, fruity wine – in the shops.

Loire wine and fruits
The Loire Valley is famous for its summery white wines and soft fruits.

Bordeaux wine
The vineyards on the banks of the Garonne River produce some of the most famous red wines in France.

Olive oil
Provence is famous for its olive oil. Traditionally, the peasants of the region ate a breakfast of bread dipped in olive oil.

Changing social habits in France have affected eating habits. Until the 1970s, women generally stayed at home to raise their children and were expected to put a big meal on the table when their husbands came home at night. There also used to be a two-hour break or longer for lunch, so people could return home at midday and have a leisurely meal before going back to work.

Today, most women go out to work and few have the time to prepare an elaborate dinner. Most people now live in cities and commute to work, so they cannot get home for lunch. To save time, many people buy pre-pared dishes, salads, sauces or desserts. The quicker pace of life has enabled US fast-food chains to open up all over France. Yet when people have the time, they love to cook for friends and family and are happy to spend time passing on tips about good restaurants.

The map above shows some of the most famous foods and wines produced in France, many of which are sold overseas.

WHAT DO THE FRENCH OWN?

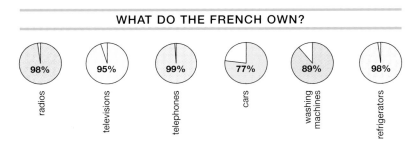

98% radios | 95% televisions | 99% telephones | 77% cars | 89% washing machines | 98% refrigerators

French households are generally well equipped with consumer goods. These charts shows the percentages of households that own some of the most common goods.

How to say ...

The French are very proud of their language. Everyday spoken French can seem very different from the the formal, sophisticated language often found in newspapers. A **state**-run organization called the Académie Française (French Academy) acts as a kind of 'language police' to defend the purity of the French language. The academy tries to limit the influence of English by attempting to ban English-derived words, such as *le weekend, le fax* and *le tennisman* (tennis player). Below are a few simple French phrases, together with a pronunciation guide. Many sounds are pronounced nasally (in the nose) – this is indicated in the pronunciation guides by square brackets ([ ]). The French also roll their r's slightly in the throat.

Please   *S'il vous plaît* (seel-voo-play)

Thank you   *Merci* (meh[re]-see)

Yes   *Oui* (wee)   No   *Non* (no[n])

Hello   *Bonjour* (boh[n]-zhur)

Goodbye   *Au revoir* (oh-rev-ooar)

See you later   *À bientôt* (ah byen-toh)

Good evening   *Bonsoir* (bo[n]-sooa[r])

Good night   *Bonne nuit* (bun-nu-ee)

How are you?   (to friends) *Ça va?* (sa-va); (to strangers) *Comment allez-vous?* (kom-mo[n]-tah-lay-voo)

Sorry   *Pardon* (par-doh[n])

Excuse me   *Excusez-moi* (ex-ku-zay-mooar

I understand   *Je comprends* (zhe-kom-pro[n])

I don't understand   *Je ne comprends pas* (zhe-ne-kom-pro[n]-pa)

Do you speak English? *Vous parlez l'anglais?* (voo-par-lay lo[n]-glay)?

What is your name?   *Comment vous-appelez-vous* (kom-o[n]-vooz-ap-play-voo)

My name is ... *Je m'appelle ...* (zhe ma-pel ...)

Sir/Mr   *Monsieur* (meh-see-yur)

Madam/Mrs   *Madame* (ma-dam)

Miss   *Mademoiselle* (ma-dam-wa-zel)

Numbers/*Nombres*:

One   *Un/une* (uh[n]/oon)

Two   *Deux*   (de[r])

Three   *Trois* (twah)

Four   *Quatre* (kat-[re])

Five   *Cinq* (sank)

Six   *Six* (sees)

Seven   *Sept* (set)

Eight   *Huit* (wee[t])

Nine   *Neuf* (nehf)

Ten   *Dix* (dees)

Days of the week/*Les jours de la semaine*:

Monday   *Lundi* (lun-dee)

Tuesday   *Mardi* (mar-dee)

Wednesday   *Mercredi* (merk-r[eh]-dee)

Thursday   *Jeudi* (zhe[r]-dee)

Friday   *Vendredi* (ve[n]-d[re]-dee)

Saturday   *Samedi* (sam-[eh]-dee)

Sunday   *Dimanche* (dee-m[on]sh)

The importance of education

Many French people grumble about the stress of exam time and the problems of their education system. In fact, the French school system is generally good and is successful at providing children with equal opportunities, whether their parents are rich or poor.

Education in France is compulsory from the ages of six to sixteen. The school year is divided into three terms, each with breaks of several days in the middle of each term. There are longer holidays at Christmas, Easter and in the summer. The state, which spends nearly one-fifth of its budget on education, runs most of the schools. Private schools are also important, and 17 per cent of school students attend private schools. Many of these are run by the Roman Catholic Church.

Most French children go to preschool and then enter primary education at the age of six, which continues until the age of eleven. The emphasis is on reading, writing, maths, geography and history. Students also have classes in physical education, art and music.

From eleven to fifteen, children go to a lower secondary school, called a *collège*. Here the curriculum broadens, homework starts to become important and teachers closely monitor the students' performance. At the age of sixteen, students may go to an upper secondary school, called a *lycée*. Those who are not academically inclined may choose to go to a *lycée professionel*, which specializes in technical training.

A French boy or girl aged seventeen or eighteen at a *lycée* focuses very hard on passing his or her secondary-school exam, known as the *baccalauréat* or *bac*. Each June, millions of households are gripped by tension and anxiety as pupils prepare for the exam, worried that if they fail, they will have to take it again. The French school system centres on the *bac*. Without this precious exam, there is no chance of going to university or of getting a well-paid job. Around ten subjects are studied for the *baccalauréat*. The idea is that students should

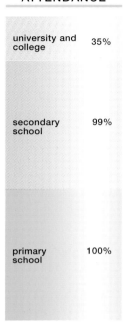

EDUCATIONAL
ATTENDANCE

university and college 35%

secondary school 99%

primary school 100%

A large number of French students remain in school beyond the age of sixteen.

Although preschool is not compulsory in France, there are some 18,000 preschools.

All in all, there are some 4900 *collèges* and 1160 *lycées* in France.

111

The Sorbonne, situated in the Latin Quarter of Paris, is one of the most prestigious universities in the world. It was founded as a religious college in about 1257 by Robert de Sorbon, from whom it gets its name.

have a well-rounded education. Specialization comes later in the French system. In their final year at the *lycée*, all students study philosophy, something that is unique to the French system.

Three paths open up for the student who has passed the *bac*. First, there are the *grandes écoles*. These 'great schools' consist of a half-dozen prestigious establishments that train France's top government officials, business managers and teachers. The entrance exam is very hard, so only a few applicants are admitted.

Second, there are the institutes of technology. These offer a two-year practical course in industry and technology. Third, there are the ordinary universities, which are open to all students who have a *baccalauréat*. After two years, a student can take a general university diploma, and after a further year, a bachelor's degree. The student can sit for a master's degree after four years, while the most gifted may get a doctorate.

There are some problems with French universities. Tuition is free, but grants for living expenses are rare, so many students have to take part-time jobs or a loan to survive. Students also complain about overcrowding and the lonely life on campus, while prospective employers often prefer work experience to academic qualifications.

Health and welfare

The French have one of the most generous social welfare systems in the world. Expenditure on welfare accounts for one-third of the country's **gross national product** (GNP). Individuals are covered for health care from the moment they are born to the day they die. The state picks up 74 per cent of the bill, while the rest is covered by private and state insurance programmes and by the individual. Hospitals are generally well equipped with the latest technology. If people lose their jobs or if their income falls below a certain level, the state provides unemployment benefit and income support.

France has one of the earliest retirement ages in the world. Men and women can leave the workforce and get a pension at the age of 60, if they have made sufficient contributions to the state retirement fund. The threshold is often lowered to 55 in the case of workers taking early retirement from troubled industries, such as steelmaking and coal mining. Most workers supplement the state pension with private investments.

The state provides the family with generous support. There are monthly cash payments geared to the number of children in the family. Families of three or more children can travel at reduced rates on public transport. Women receive a long paid maternity leave, and there is daycare for the children of single parents if the parents want to go to work.

Holidays and recreation

Never have the French had an easier life. Paid holidays are getting longer, the working week is getting shorter and industries have sprung up to cater to people with leisure time on their hands. Over the past century, the legal working week has been

National holidays and festivals

1 January	Jour de l'an/ New Year's Day
March/April	Pâques/ Easter Sunday
March/April	Lundi de Pâques/ Easter Monday
1 May	Fête du Travail/ Labour Day
8 May	Victoire 1945/ Victory Day for World War Two
May	Ascension/ Ascension Day
May to June	Lundi de Pentecôte/ Pentecost Sunday
14 July	Fête nationale/ Bastille Day
15 August	Assomption/ Assumption Day
1 November	Toussaint/ All Saints' Day
11 November	Fête de l'armistice 1918/Armistice Day 1918
25 December	Nöel/ Christmas Day

French school children have five holidays:

- **Christmas (13 days)**
- **winter (15 days)**
- **spring (15 days)**
- **summer (68 days)**
- **All Saints (8 days)**

reduced from 48 hours to 35 hours. Employees now get a minimum of five weeks' paid holiday, but long-serving employees usually get an extra week or two.

Added to paid holidays are thirteen national holidays, ranging from New Year's Day to feast days in the Roman Catholic calendar. National Day is 14 July, which celebrates the storming of the **Bastille** prison in Paris in 1789. Despite the decline of religion and nationalism in France over the past century, everybody still celebrates these holidays by taking time off.

The French spend much of their free time at home, watching television or gardening, or going on holiday. At the start of the school summer holiday in July, hundreds of thousands of people leave Paris and other large cities and head for the sunny beaches on the Mediterranean or the Atlantic. Families often try to leave before dawn to beat the rush, only to find that everyone else has done the same.

Religion in France

More than four-fifths of the population of France describe themselves as Roman Catholics. Religion, however, plays a minor role in everyday life. The great majority of Roman Catholics do not go to church regularly, and many people ignore the church's dictates on abortion, contraception, divorce, homosexuality and premarital sex.

Many people also say they have no opinion about whether there is a God or claim they are atheists (non-believers). However, schools run by the church play a prominent part in the education system, but they have to keep to a curriculum set down by the government.

The decline of the church's influence dates back centuries, as people became disillusioned with the abuse of power by priests and bishops. This started an anti-religion movement that culminated in 1905, when Catholicism lost its status as France's official religion.

US banknotes declare 'In God We Trust', but French banknotes never bore such a motto. French people generally believe that the state should not make declarations of faith.

Today, the fastest-growing religion in France is Islam because of the influx of Muslim immigrants from Algeria, Tunisia and Morocco.

Many people in France are sport enthusiasts. Millions follow the Tour de France bicycle race each year. The race takes place over much of France in July, and the final stage is always held on the Avenue des Champs-Elysées in Paris.

The Tour de France is the most famous bicycle race in the world. The race was created in 1903 by Henri Desgranges.

Football (soccer), too, has always been a popular sport, and in 1998, France won the World Cup. Rugby is very popular in the south and south-west. The finals of the football and rugby championships are played in Paris, in the national stadium.

During the summer, the French version of bowls is popular among older people. Known as *pétanque* in the south and as *boules* in the north, the game is played on gravel areas in town parks or village squares. Also popular are skiing, judo, golf and sailing. Going to the cinema is another popular way of spending an evening.

A changing lifestyle

Twenty years ago, people in France would typically buy their goods at different shops in a few streets close to where they lived. Most of the shops were closed on Sundays, except for the bakery. Neighbourhood shops still exist, but they are losing ground to supermarkets. Massive sales outlets called *hypermarchés*, built on the outskirts of towns, comprise a shopping mall in one store.

The change in shopping habits reflects France's own shift from a largely rural society to a suburban one. The outskirts of most cities now consist of high-rise apartment blocks or housing estates. The people who live there commute to work by train, bus or car. Critics say that the suburbs lack not only the character of the city centre but also the friendliness of the countryside. In some high-rise housing estates, called **HLMs**, in the suburbs around Paris, Lyon and Marseille, there are problems with violence and ethnic tension.

Traditional French shops include:
- **the bakery** (*boulangerie-pâtisserie*) for a baguette and croissants
- **the grocer** (*épicerie*)
- **the fishmonger** (*poissonnerie*)
- **the butcher** (*boucherie*).

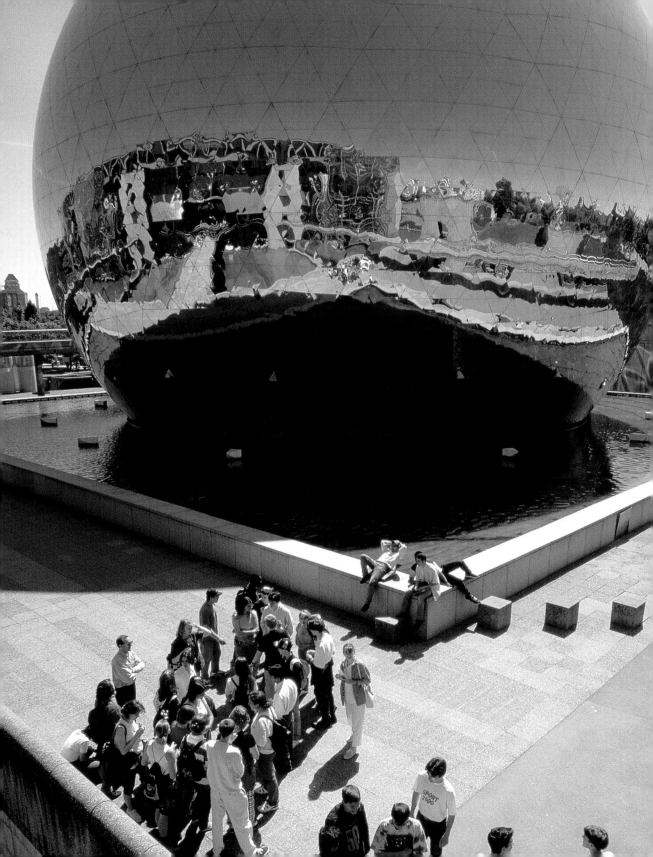

The future

'Il faut cultiver notre jardin.' [We have to cultivate our garden.]

Closing line of *Candide*, a novel by 18th-century
French writer and philosopher Voltaire

A look at France's beautiful landscape, a taste of its wonderful food and a glimpse at its glorious past might cause anyone to think that this is a happy, untroubled country. But that is far from the truth. France today is going through a difficult time as it faces major challenges at home and abroad. Many French people are uncertain and anxious about the future.

THE DECLINE OF AN EMPIRE

The mood is so sombre that France – traditionally a country where immigrants come to look for a new life – has recently become a land of emigration. Young French people, fed up with a gloomy life without a job, leave to find work abroad. Today, more than 220,000 French people live in the USA. The next largest groups live in Britain, Germany, Belgium and Switzerland.

The past hundred years have not been kind to France's self-esteem. A century ago, France was a leading colonial power. It was a cultural giant with a capital city that bubbled over with life. The French language was used internationally. Today, however, France is a middle-ranking power struggling with the legacy of colonization. Even its culture has lost some of its vibrancy, and globally its language has lost ground to English and Spanish.

At home, the French economy needs to undergo the kind of painful overhaul that many of its competitors

France continues to create fresh and striking ideas. The Géode – a polished, 36-metre-high (120-foot) sphere – dominates the Parc des Sciences, Paris.

faced in the 1980s. The country is bound by tight regulation and government control. This can dampen entrepreneurial spirit in France and means that citizens sometimes expect solutions from the government rather than looking for their own.

The private sector of the economy remains strong but is burdened by heavy taxation and high labour costs. Many companies are moving their factories and offices to other countries where production costs are lower. The **state** sector, which absorbs a lot of money from public funds, is in even greater need of reform. The difficulty is that reform could mean the loss of thousands of jobs. The welfare system is so expensive that, without major cuts in spending, it could face collapse.

These are the problems that governments have ignored for years, fearing an angry response from trade unions or mass protests in the street. As the problems grow, so do crime, vandalism and the jobless rate. Unemployment particularly strikes young people leaving school and manual workers. These people have become susceptible to the ideas of **right-wing** extremists, who seek to inflame racial tension by blaming unemployment on France's large community of North African immigrants.

A chef in a Tunisian restaurant in Paris prepares food typical of his country. The French capital is increasingly multi-ethnic, creating both pleasures and problems for its people.

THE NEW MILLENNIUM

Despite these difficulties, France enjoys many advantages. It is currently enjoying one of the longest periods of peace in its history. It has no border disputes, and war with its traditional enemy, Germany, is unthinkable. The agricultural sector is strong and France has a well-educated workforce. It may lag behind its competitors in retailing and finance, but is successful in vehicle construction and utilities such as power plants. Global co-operation has enabled it to develop a good skills base in aircraft-making, rail transportation and space rockets.

France has enjoyed an unparalleled period of stability over the past half century. Yet the tradition of strong public protest still survives. The tensions that this creates in society have caused difficulties since the French Revolution. The new century requires a government that can carry out reforms, although many of these may not be popular with the public. The coming years could be a stern test for the institutions of the Fifth Republic, at a time when many people have a low opinion of politicians and political parties.

Much will depend on the great gamble of the European Monetary Union (EMU). If the single currency issued by the union succeeds, the nationalist tension that caused wars between France and its neighbours for centuries may be at an end. The economy would get a big boost, and unemployment would decline.

If, however, the single currency fails, causes **inflation** or plunges the country into recession, there could be a backlash against the process of European integration. People may insist on the restoration of the French franc and on the reimposition of barriers to foreign trade, even against France's partners in the European Union. If that happened, the foundations of France's modern prosperity could be at risk.

But France is a resilient country. Throughout its history, it has suffered through war and revolution. Nevertheless, its people have always been able to draw strength from the tragedies and crises that have shaken their country and to re-create France anew.

The map above shows those countries of the European Union that joined the European Monetary Union (EMU) in 1999.

The future of France is closely bound up with that of the European Union, whose flag is shown below. But will France be able to hold its own in an enlarged EU, as more countries join?

Almanac

POLITICAL

country name:
official form: the French Republic
short form: France
local official form: *La République
    Française*
local short form: *La France*

nationality:
> noun: Frenchman/woman
> adjective: French

official language: French

capital city: Paris

type of government: republic

suffrage (voting rights): everyone
    eighteen years and over

overseas territories:
> French Guiana, French Polynesia, Guadeloupe,
> Martinique, Mayotte, New Caledonia,
> Réunion, St Pierre & Miquelon and
> Wallis & Fortuna

national anthem: 'La Marseillaise'

national day: 14 July (Bastille Day)

Flag:

GEOGRAPHICAL

location: western Europe; latitudes
    42.5° to 51° north and
    longitudes 5° west to 8° east

climate: France has three types
    of climate: oceanic (west),
    Mediterranean (south) and
    continental (centre and east)

total area: 551,204 sq km
    (212,820 sq miles)
land: 99.7%
water: 0.3%

coastline: 3700 km (2300 miles)

terrain: mostly flat plains or
    gently rolling hills in the
    north and west; the remainder
    is mountainous, especially
    the Pyrenees in the south
    and the Alps in the south-east

highest point: Mont Blanc,
    4807 m (15,771 ft)
lowest point: Rhône River delta,
    −1 m (−3 ft)

natural resources: coal, iron ore,
    bauxite, fish, timber, zinc
    and potash

land use:

    arable land: 32%

    forests and woodland: 27%

    meadows and pasture: 23%

    permanent crops: 2%

    other: 16%

natural hazards: flooding

POPULATION

population (2001 est.): 59.5 million

population growth rate (2001 est.):
    0.37%

birth rate (2001 est.): 12.1 births
    per 1000 of the population

death rate (2001 est.): 9.09 deaths
    per 1000 of the population

sex ratio (2001 est.): 95 males per
    100 females

total fertility rate (2001 est.): 175
    children born for every 1000
    women in the population

infant mortality rate (2001 est.):
    4.46 deaths per 1000 live births

life expectancy at birth (2001 est.):
    total population: 78.9 years
    male: 75.01 years
    female: 83.01 years

literacy:

    total population: 99%

    male: 99%

    female: 99%

ECONOMY

currency: euro (€);
    €1 = 100 cents

exchange rate (2002):
    £1 = €1.6

gross national product (2001 est.):
    £943,750 million (fifth-largest
    economy in the world)

average annual growth rate
    (1990–9): 1.5%

GNP per capita (2002 est.): £15,875

average annual inflation rate
    (1990–2000): 4.2%

unemployment rate (2001 est.): 8.9%

exports (2001 est.): £183,313 million
imports (2001 est.): £182,875 million

foreign aid given (1999): £3525 million

Human Development Index
(an index scaled from 0 to 100 combining statistics
indicating adult literacy, years of schooling, life
expectancy and income levels):
    91.7 (UK 91.8)

TIMELINE – FRANCE

 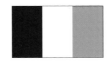

World history

French history

c.15,000 BC

c.14,000
Birth of El-Kebareh civilization in Israel

c.15,000 Lascaux cave paintings are created in south-west France

c.1500 BC

753 Traditional date of the foundation of Rome

492–479 Wars between Persia and Greek city-states

c.1500 Gauls migrate to France from central Europe

390 Gauls sack Rome

52 BC Romans conquer Gaul (France)

c.AD 300

306 Constantine becomes Roman emperor and legalizes Christianity

900 Vikings land in North America

486 Frankish leader Clovis defeats the Roman governor of France

800 The pope crowns Charlemagne emperor of the Holy Roman empire

1453 Turks capture Constantinople

1445 Gutenberg prints the first European book

1348 Black Death breaks out in Europe

1337–1453 The Hundred Years' War

1066 Normans conquer Britain

c.1000

1642–51 The English Civil War

1520 Birth of Protestantism – the pope expels Martin Luther from the Roman Catholic Church

1643 Louis XIV (the 'Sun King') becomes king

1589 The last Valois king is assassinated and the Bourbon dynasty begins

1572 Huguenots (French Protestants) are massacred in Paris

c.1500

1453 The Hundred Years' War ends

1429 Joan of Arc inspires a French victory at Orléans

1415 English defeat the French at the Battle of Agincourt

1328 Accession of Valois dynasty triggers outbreak of Hundred Years' War against England

c.1700

1740–8 War of the Austrian Succession

***c.*1750** Industrial Revolution begins in Britain

1789 Revolution breaks out in France

1793 King Louis XVI is executed

1799 Napoleon Bonaparte is proclaimed First Consul of the Republic

2000 The West celebrates the Millennium – 2000 years since the birth of Christ

2002 The euro replaces the franc as the French national currency

c.2000

1989 Communism collapses in eastern Europe. The fall of the Berlin Wall.

1963–75 Vietnam War

1962 Algeria gains its independence

1954 Revolt breaks out in Algeria

1995 Chirac becomes president

1968 Students riot in Paris

1958 The Fifth Republic begins with de Gaulle as president

1957 France joins the European Economic Community (EEC), later the European Union (EU)

c.1800

1803 Britain declares war on France

1853–6 The Crimean War

1870–1 Franco-Prussian War

1871 Bismarck unites German states into a single country

1899–1902 The Boer War

1804 Napoleon crowns himself emperor of France

1814 Britain and Prussia occupy France. Napoleon is exiled to Elba.

1815 Napoleon is defeated at Waterloo

1851 Second Empire begins under Napoleon III

1871 Prussia defeats France. The Commune is suppressed.

1894–1900 Dreyfus affair divides France

c. 1950

1944 The Allies liberate France

1940 Germany invades France

1919 Treaty of Versailles punishes Germany

1914 Germany invades France

1939–45 World War Two

1933 Adolf Hitler becomes German chancellor

1914–18 World War One

c.1900

Glossary

ancien régime (Fr. 'old order') social and governmental system of France before the 1789 revolution

autoroute toll motorway

basilica large Roman Catholic church

Bastille 18th-century prison in Paris, destroyed during the French Revolution

capital goods raw materials that are used to produce other goods – for example, the steel needed to produce a car

château castle or large country house

conservatism political philosophy based on maintaining tradition and stability

constitution fundamental principles that underlie the government of a country

constitutional monarchy monarchy that rules according to a Constitution

consumer goods manufactured goods ready for sale directly to the public – for example, cars and clothes

cordillera system of mountain ranges

département (Fr.) second-largest administrative unit into which France is divided. There are 96 *départements* in metropolitan France.

dirigisme (Fr.) government policy of planning and controlling the economy

ecology study of the relationships between animals, plants, humans and the environment

euro unit of the single European currency

Existentialism philosophical and literary movement based on the doctrine that human beings are totally free and responsible for their actions

exports goods sold by one country to another

foreign debt money owed by a nation to the rest of the world

gross national product (GNP) total value of goods and services produced by the people of a country during a period, usually a year

HLM (Fr. 'habitation à loyer modéré' – home with a moderate rent) high-rise housing in an urban area

hydroelectricity electricity produced by harnessing the water power of rivers

imports goods bought by one country from another

inflation annual rate at which prices increase in a country

La Bourse (Fr.) Paris stock exchange

Latin language of ancient Rome; later used by priests and scholars

left wing political position characterized by socialist or communist views

Légion d'Honneur (Fr.) France's highest civilian award

lycée (Fr.) upper secondary school for students aged sixteen and over

lycée professionnel (Fr.) technical training college attended by less academically inclined students

maquis (Fr.) dense scrubland; also the name for the French Resistance fighters during World War Two

Marianne personification of the French Republic

massif compact group of eroded mountains

métro (Fr.) Paris underground train system

monarchy form of government in which a monarch – king or queen – is head of state

national debt money owed by a nation because of loans made to it

nation-state modern nation as the main unit of political organization

nouveau roman (Fr. 'new novel') form of writing that abandons traditional aspects of the novel, such as plot and identifiable characters

Nouvelle Vague (Fr. 'New Wave') style of film that emerged in the 1950s, characterized by techniques such as jump cuts and improvised dialogue

prehistory time before written or recorded history

principality territory ruled by a prince or princess

radicalism political philosophy that promotes extreme change in society – for example, by revolution

Realism 19th-century art movement that aimed to represent the world as it was

Renaissance great revival of the arts in Europe in the 15th and 16th centuries that looked back to the examples of ancient Greece and Rome

right wing conservative political philosophy

sans-culottes (Fr. 'without breeches') members of the republican faction during the French Revolution

state government of a country or nation

Terror period of repression and violence (1793–4) during the French Revolution

tricolore (Fr. 'tricolour') flag of France, so named because it has three bands of blue, white and red

Bibliography

Major sources used for this book
Ardagh, John, *France in the New Century: Portrait of a Changing Society* (Viking, 1999)
Doyle, William, *The Oxford History of the French Revolution* (Oxford University Press, 2002)
The Economist *Pocket World in Figures* (Profile Books, 1998)
France, Peter, (ed.) *The New Oxford Companion to Literature in French* (Oxford University Press, 1995)
Robertson, Ian, *Blue Guides: France* (WW Norton, 1997)
Zeldin, Theodore, *The French* (Collins Harvill, 1988)

General further reading
Clawson, Elmer, *Activities and Investigations in Economics* (Addison-Wesley, 1994)
The DK Geography of the World (Dorling Kindersley, 1996)
The Kingfisher History Encyclopedia (Kingfisher, 1999)
Martell, Hazel M, *The Kingfisher Book of the Ancient World* (Kingfisher, 1995)
Student Atlas (Dorling Kindersley, 1998)

Further reading about France
Ardagh, John, and Colin Jones, *The Cultural Atlas of France* (Facts on File, 1991)
Biel, Timothy L, *The Importance of Charlemagne* (Lucent Books: 1997)
Hugo, Victor, *The Hunchback of Notre-Dame* (New American Library, 1982)
Jones, Colin, and Emmanuel Le Roy, *The Cambridge Illustrated History of France* (Cambridge University Press, 1999)
Stein, R. Conrad, *Paris* (Children's Press, 1997)

Some websites about France
www.travel-guide.com/data/fra/fra001.asp
www.countryreports.org/france.htm

Index

Acknowledgements

Cover photo credit
Corbis: Owen Franken

Photo credits
AKG Photo: 56, 59, 74; **ADAGP, Paris and DACS, London 1999:** 98; **Bridgeman Art Library:** Giraudon 58; **Citroën Public Affairs:** 84; **Bruce Coleman:** John Cancalosi 35; Staffan Widstrand 34; **Corbis:** Bettmann 69, 104, 105; Gianni Dagli Orti 48, 50, 100; Owen Franken 118; Franz-Marc Frei 47; Robert Holmes 116; Angelo Hornak 92; Hulton-Deutsch Collection 103; Library of Congress 54; Francis G. Mayer 97; Patrick Ward 96; Michael S. Yamashita 112; **Mary Evans:** Explorer 55; **Hulton Getty:** 64; **Robert Hunt Library:** 65, 70; **Hutchison Library:** Jeremy Horner 81; Christine Pemberton 38; **Image Bank:** Marvin E. Newman 40; F. Hidalgo 44 tr; Hans Wolf 83; **Image Select:** 101; Ann Ronan 60, 63; **Life File:** Andrew Ward 53, 82; **NHPA:** Henry Ausloos 28; Nina Ricci 90; **TRH Pictures:** 67; **Tony Stone Images:** Michael Busselle 20, 29, 108; Tony Craddock 12; David Epperson 6; Suzanne and Nick Geary 43; Cris Haigh 95; David Hughes 25; Patrick Ingrand 16; Chris Kapolka 88; Sally Mayman 26; Martine Mouchy 19; Richard Passmore 85, 106; Jake Rajs 31; Eric Renard 115; Bertrand Rieger 76; Stephen Studd 22; Charlie Waite 27; Jeremy Walker 36; Gavin Hellier 44bl.